The Middle East

Volume 5
TURKEY • UNITED ARAB EMIRATES • YEMEN

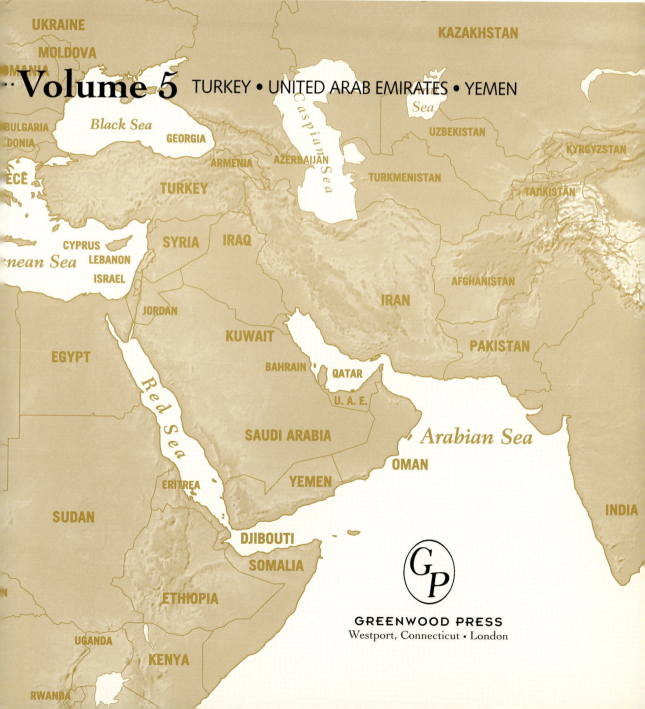

Discovering World Cultures

The Middle East

Volume 5   TURKEY • UNITED ARAB EMIRATES • YEMEN

GREENWOOD PRESS
Westport, Connecticut • London

Library of Congress Cataloging-in-Publication Data

Discovering world cultures: the Middle East / by Creative Media Applications.
    p. cm. — (Middle school reference)
      Contents: v. 1. Bahrain, Cyprus, Egypt — v. 2. Iran, Iraq, Israel — v. 3. Jordan, Kuwait, Lebanon,
    Oman — v. 4. Qatar, Saudi Arabia, Syria — v. 5. Turkey, United Arab Emirates, Yemen.
      Includes bibliographical references and index.
      ISBN 0–313–32922–2 (set: alk. paper) — ISBN 0–313–32923–0 (v. 1: alk.paper) —
      ISBN 0–313–32924–9 (v. 2: alk. paper) — ISBN 0–313–32925–7 (v. 3: alk. paper) —
      ISBN 0–313–32926–5 (v. 4: alk. paper) — ISBN 0–313–32927–3 (v. 5: alk. paper)
        1. Ethnology — Middle East. 2. Middle East — Social life and customs. I. Creative Media Applications.
        II. Series.
    GN635.N42D57   2004
    306.'0956 — dc22   2003044263

British Library Cataloguing in Publication Data is available.

Library of Congress Catalog Card Number: 2003044263
ISBN: 0–313–32922–2 (set)
       0–313–32923–0 (vol. 1)
       0–313–32924–9 (vol. 2)
       0–313–32925–7 (vol. 3)
       0–313–32926–5 (vol. 4)
       0–313–32927–3 (vol. 5)

First published in 2004

Greenwood Press, 88 Post Road West, Westport, CT 06881
An imprint of Greenwood Publishing Group, Inc.
www.greenwood.com

Printed in the United States of America

∞
The paper used in this book complies with the Permanent Paper Standard
issued by the National Information Standards Organization (Z39.48–1984).

10 9 8 7 6 5 4 3 2 1

A Creative Media Applications, Inc. Production
WRITER: Sandy Pobst
DESIGN AND PRODUCTION: Alan Barnett, Inc.
EDITOR: Susan Madoff
COPYEDITOR: Laurie Lieb
PROOFREADER: Betty Pessagno
INDEXER: Nara Wood
ASSOCIATED PRESS PHOTO RESEARCHER: Yvette Reyes
CONSULTANT: Abraham Marcus is Associate Professor of Middle Eastern History and
    former Director of the Center for Middle Eastern Studies at the University of Texas at Austin.

PHOTO CREDITS:
AP/Wide World Photographs pages: x, 2, 4, 6, 9, 10, 19, 22, 31, 32, 39, 40, 45, 48, 55, 61, 64, 65, 67, 68, 74, 76, 78, 83,
    88, 92, 96, 99, 101, 108, 111, 112
© Yves Herman/Reuters /Landov page: 14
© Nik Wheeler/CORBIS page: 25
© Hulton Archives/Getty Images page: 26
© Bettmann/CORBIS pages: 35, 36
© Fatih Saribas/Reuters/Landov page: 43
© Kerim Okten/EPA /Landov page: 51
© Vanni Archive/CORBIS page: 56
© Chris Hellier/CORBIS page: 58
© Gianni Dagli Orti/CORBIS page: 71
© Aladin Abdel Naby/REUTERS/Landov page: 93
© Ali Jarekji/Landov page: 95
© Archivo Iconografico, S.A./CORBIS page: 100
© Dietmar Jedziny/DPA/Landov page: 102, 105
© Ingolf Muller/DPA/Landov page: 114

Table of Contents

Thanks to Linda Miller Raff, Mary Ann Segalla,
and Amy Snyder for their contributions.

INTRODUCTION

The Middle East. The name conjures up many different images for most Westerners: fascinating ancient civilizations, the rise and fall of powerful empires, and—most recently—bloody conflicts and suicide bombers. This series introduces the history, customs, and cultures of the people living in the Middle East in the hope of inspiring a fuller understanding of a complex region.

What Is the Middle East?

"The Middle East" is a rather vague name for such an important region of the world. What is it in the middle of? And how is it different from the Near East and the Far East?

Most of the geographical terms used in the world today, such as the label "Middle East," originated with Europeans and Americans. As Europeans explored the world around them, they first headed east. The lands that bordered the eastern basin of the Mediterranean Sea—Anatolia (Turkey), Syria, Palestine, and Egypt, as well as their immediate neighbors—became known as the "Near East." Countries farther away, such as China and Indonesia, were referred to as the "Far East."

The term "Middle East" has been in use for only the past century. It was first used by an American military officer to describe the geopolitical

MEASURING TIME

Most of the world today uses the Gregorian calendar, which is based on the solar year. Because it is a Christian calendar, historical dates have traditionally been designated as occurring before the birth of Christ (B.C.) or after the birth of Christ (A.D., an acronym for the Latin phrase *Anno Domini,* meaning "in the year of the Lord"). In recent years, historians have started to use neutral, nonreligious terms to describe these divisions of time. The *Discovering World Cultures: The Middle East* series follows this practice, using B.C.E. (before the Common Era) rather than B.C. and C.E. (Common Era) in place of A.D. (Some people define the terms as "Before the Christian Era" and "Christian Era.") The dating system remains the same: 1000 B.C. is the same as 1000 B.C.E., while 2003 C.E. is the same as A.D. 2003.

region that included the countries between the Mediterranean Sea and India—those countries in the middle of the Eastern Hemisphere that shared a common culture. Today, there are many different definitions of the Middle East. Some scholars include the countries of northern Africa in their definition of the Middle East. Others use a cultural definition that includes all the predominantly Islamic countries in Africa and Asia. This series adopts the definition used by most modern scholars, adding Egypt to the original list of Middle Eastern countries because of its shared history and Arabic culture.

Birthplace of World Religions

As home to the world's earliest civilizations, the Middle East is also the birthplace of three of the world's major religions: Judaism, Christianity, and Islam. Followers of these three religions worship the same god and share a common early history. Today, about 2 billion people worldwide identify themselves as Christian, while about 1.3 billion follow Islam. Nearly 14 million are Jews. Together, these three groups make up 53 percent of the world's population.

Judaism

Judaism is the oldest of the three religions, originating nearly 4,000 years ago in the land of Israel (also known as Palestine). Jews believe that Abraham, who was born in Ur in present-day Iraq, was the founder of Judaism. About 1800 B.C.E., he began to teach that the world was created by a single god. God made a covenant, or agreement, with Abraham: if Abraham left his home and followed God's commandments, God would bless Abraham with children and establish a great nation. Moses, a descendant of Abraham's son Isaac, later led the Jewish people out of slavery in Egypt. God made a new covenant with Moses, providing instructions and rules for living a holy life, including the Ten Commandments.

According to Jewish tradition, Abraham's first son, Ishmael, is the ancestor of the Arab people. His second son, Isaac, is the ancestor of the Jewish people.

Jews believe that when they follow the Torah—the first five books of the Hebrew Bible, or holy book—and keep God's laws, the Jewish people and the nation of Israel will be blessed by God. They also believe that God will send a Messiah, a political leader chosen by God to bring the

Jewish *exiles* back to Israel, rebuild Jerusalem and restore the Temple that was destroyed by the Romans in 70 c.e., and put an end to the evil in the world. (For more information about Judaism, please see page 108 in Volume 2.)

Christianity

Christianity grew out of Judaism about 2,000 years ago in Israel when Jesus Christ, a Jewish man, began teaching about faith and God's love. Christians believe that Jesus Christ is the son of God, the Messiah sent by God to save people from sin and death. They believe that Jesus was resurrected after his death and that, through faith, they too will have life after death. The Christian Bible includes both the Hebrew Bible (Old Testament) and the teachings of Jesus and his disciples (the New Testament). Unlike Jews and Muslims, Christians believe in the Trinity of God—that God exists as the Father, the Son, and the Holy Spirit. (For more information about Christianity, please see pages 56–60 in Volume 1 of *Discovering World Cultures: The Middle East*.)

Islam

Islam was founded in the seventh century by the Prophet Mohammad, who was a direct descendant of Ishmael. Muslims believe in only one god, Allah, the same god worshiped by Jews and Christians. According to Islamic tradition, Allah's message to humans has been delivered by prophets, such as Abraham, Moses, Jesus, and Mohammad. Holy books, including the Torah, the Christian Gospels, and the Qur'an, preserve the word of Allah. Because the countries in the Middle East are predominantly Islamic, a detailed overview of Islam is provided here.

Basic Beliefs

Muslims believe that the "five pillars of Islam" are the key to salvation:

- *Shahadah:* the acknowledgment that "there is no god but God and that Mohammad is the messenger of God"
- *Salah:* five daily ritual prayers
- *Zakat:* the giving of money to the poor
- *Sawm:* the dawn-to-dusk fast during the month of Ramadan, Islam's most important religious observance
- *Hajj:* the pilgrimage to Mecca, the birthplace of Mohammad

Forms of Islam

About 85 percent of the Islamic community follows the Sunni tradition (in Arabic, *Sunni* refers to the people who follow the sunna, or example, of the prophet). Sunni Muslims believe that the *caliph,* or spiritual leader, should be chosen by the consensus of the Islamic community. They also believe that following *shari'a,* or Islamic, law is essential in living a life that ends in salvation.

The Shi'a tradition teaches that Mohammad appointed his cousin and son-in-law Ali and his descendants to be the spiritual and worldly leaders of Islam after Mohammad's death. Shi'ite (SHE-ite) Muslims believe that these leaders, called *imams,* are free of sin and infallible. About 15 percent of all Muslims follow Shi'a Islam, but there are several different branches within the Shi'a tradition.

Wahhabism is an Islamic reform movement that originated in the eighteenth century in Saudi Arabia. Its members are the most conservative, fundamentalist group in Islam. Members reject any

Iraqi Shi'ite Muslims gather at a holy site in the city of Karbala, Iraq, in April 2003, to mourn the death of one of their most important saints. Under the rule of Iraqi leader Saddam Hussein, they had been banned from observing such rituals for decades. With Hussein's fall from power that same month, however, they were free to worship.

modern interpretations of Islam, including the celebration of Mohammad's birthday or playing music. Muslims who adopt Wahhabi principles label those who don't share their beliefs as infidels or unbelievers, even those who are moderate Sunnis and Shi'ites.

Sources of Muslim Teachings and Tradition

The Qur'an is the only holy book of the Islam faith. Muslims believe that the Qur'an contains the literal word of Allah, or God, which was revealed to the Prophet Mohammad. Memorizing and reciting these holy words is an important part of daily prayer and worship. (Many Americans refer to this book as the Koran, a Westernized spelling of Qur'an.)

While the Qur'an is the only holy text, there are other important spiritual sources in the Islamic faith. The Sunna is a collection of all the stories, sayings, and actions of Mohammad. Followers of Islam use these examples to determine correct behavior in areas not covered in the Qur'an. They often come up with different explanations, which is why customs and beliefs vary sometimes from group to group. One of the distinct features of Islam is the Shari'a, a comprehensive body of laws covering personal, civil, and criminal matters.

COURTESY AND CUSTOMS IN THE MIDDLE EAST

Middle Eastern customs and traditions have developed over centuries, influenced by tribal culture and religion. Visitors to the region should be aware of rules and taboos, such as the ones shown here, that apply in most Middle Eastern countries.

- When greeting a man, clasp his hand briefly without shaking it. A man should never move to shake hands with a woman unless she offers her hand first. Inquiries about an acquaintance's health and interests are expected, but you should never ask about a Muslim's female family members.

- Showing the sole of your shoe to another person, such as when you sit with one leg crossed over the other knee, is very rude. The soles of your shoes should always be pointing downward.

- Always offer and receive items with your right hand. If you are served a meal in a traditional manner, use your right hand for eating (the left hand is regarded as unclean).

- When you visit a person's home, compliments about the home are welcome, but avoid admiring or praising an item excessively. The host may feel obligated to give the item to you as a gift.

- Photographing people is viewed with suspicion in some areas. It is important to ask permission before photographing anyone, especially a woman.

Major Religious Holidays

- *Ashura:* The first ten days of the New Year are a period of mourning for Shi'ite Muslims as they remember the assassination of Hussein, grandson of the Prophet Mohammad, in 680 C.E.

- *Ramadan:* Ramadan honors the time when Mohammad received the first of the Qur'an from Allah. It is the ninth and most holy month in the Islamic year. Muslims do not eat or drink from dawn until dusk during Ramadan. Instead, they reflect on their relationship with Allah, asking for forgiveness for their sins.

- *Eid al-Fitr:* As Ramadan ends, Muslims gather with family and friends to celebrate the feast of Eid al-Fitr. Children often get new clothes for the holiday, which usually lasts three days. Gifts are exchanged among friends and family.

- *Eid al-Adha:* Eid al-Adha (the Feast of the Sacrifice) honors the Prophet Abraham and his devotion to God. At the end of the hajj, the pilgrimage to Mecca, an animal is sacrificed, and the meat is divided between family members and the poor.

A Final Note

Transcribing the Arabic language into English often creates confusion. The two alphabets are very different and there is not a direct correlation of sounds. As a result, Arabic words are often given several different spellings in Western writing. One source may refer to the *emir* of a region, while another labels the ruler an *amir*. The name of the prophet who established Islam appears as Mohammad, Muhammad, and Mohammed. The Islamic holy book is the Qur'an or Koran, and so on. Another source of confusion is the different place names used by Westerners and those who live in the Middle East. For instance, the body of water between Iraq and the Arabian Peninsula has been called the Persian Gulf for centuries by Westerners. People living nearby, however, refer to it as the Arabian Gulf. In this series, the most commonly used spellings and the labels most familiar to Westerners have been used in an effort to avoid confusion. The exception lies in the spelling of *Qur'an,* the Islamic holy book, since scholars as well as many Muslims prefer that spelling over the Westernized *Koran*.

Turkey

The northernmost country in the Middle East, Turkey straddles the Bosporus (BAHS-pur-us)—the strait that divides the continents of Europe and Asia. Because of its location, Anatolia (the Asian mainland of Turkey) has long been the passageway between Europe, Asia, and Africa. Trade and migration routes across Asia carried Turks from Central Asia into Anatolia, where they quickly rose to power. The seas surrounding much of Turkey also brought both trade and conquerors to its shores. Today, the clear waters and beautiful beaches along Turkey's Aegean and Mediterranean shores attract thousands of tourists each year.

The Turks

During the rule of the Ottoman Empire, the area of present-day Turkey included many different ethnic and religious groups. Greeks, Armenians, Circassians, Kurds, Arabs, and Turks all had sizable communities in Thrace and Anatolia, as did other ethnic groups. Today, most people living in Turkey are ethnic Turks, Kurds, or Arabs. Small communities of other ethnic groups still remain, although most are steadily decreasing in size.

Since the emergence of the Republic of Turkey in 1923, the government has worked to replace its citizens' ethnic and religious identities with a Turkish national identity in order to promote a unified

FAST FACTS

✔ **Official name:** Republic of Turkey

✔ **Capital:** Ankara

✔ **Location:** Borders the Mediterranean Sea north of Syria and south of Greece; straddles Europe and Asia

✔ **Area:** 301,384 square miles (780,580 square kilometers)

✔ **Population:** 68,109,469 (July 2002 estimate)

✔ **Age distribution:**
0–14 years: 27%
15–64 years: 67%
over 65 years: 6%

✔ **Life expectancy:**
Males: 69 years
Females: 74 years

✔ **Ethnic groups:** Turkish 80%, Kurdish 17%, Arab 2%, other 1%

✔ **Religions:** Muslim 99.8%, other 0.2% (mostly Christians and Jews)

✔ **Languages:** Turkish, Kurdish, Arabic, Armenian, Greek

✔ **Currency:**
Turkish lira (TRL)
US$1 = 1,371,126 TRL

✔ **Average annual income:** US$2,530

✔ **Major exports:** Fruit, vegetables, textiles, clothing, iron, and steel

Source: CIA, *The World Factbook 2002;* BBC News Country Profiles.

society. Laws were passed to restrict the use and teaching of languages other than Turkish. Historical records were interpreted in a manner that benefited the government's efforts, as in the case of the Kurds, whom the government labeled as Mountain Turks rather than as an ethnic minority. This effort to erase ethnic affiliation met with limited success, and in recent years, the government has relaxed its restrictions against non-Turkish ethnic celebrations and the speaking of languages other than Turkish in public.

Did You Know?

With just over 68 million people, Turkey is the second most populous nation in the Middle East, behind Egypt.

Turks

Ethnic Turks are the largest population group in modern Turkey. They include peoples who came to the region at different times and from different places. Some are the descendants of the Turkish tribes and armies of central Asian origin who won Anatolia from the Byzantines in battle in the medieval period. Many others are the descendants of the Greek and Armenian populations of Anatolia who converted to Islam and adopted the Turkish language in the aftermath of the Turkish conquest.

Many Turks have their origins in the numerous migrations of people into the area over the centuries. When the Ottoman Empire lost its territories in Europe (known as Rumelia) in the course of the nineteenth and early twentieth centuries, many of the Turks and Muslims living in those areas fled their homes to escape persecution. Most resettled in Anatolia. The area of present-day Turkey also became populated with many speakers of Turkic languages from central Asia immigrating in the wake of the Russian conquest of their lands. The immigrants included some who were not ethnic Turks, such as Muslim Circassians from the Caucasus Mountains in Russia and Muslims from Bosnia and Albania. These groups assimilated quickly into Turkish society, intermarrying with ethnic Turks and adopting the Turkish language. Muslim

A COUNTRY BY ANY OTHER NAME

Modern Turkey includes regions whose ancient geographical names are still in use. These regional names include all or part of present-day Turkey.

Thrace	the part of Turkey that lies in Europe	Asia Minor	the peninsula that is bordered by the Black Sea, the Sea of Marmara, the Aegean Sea, and the Mediterranean Sea
Anatolia	the part of Turkey that lies in Asia		

immigrants are still welcome in Turkey today. Most come from countries that were once under the control of the Ottoman Empire or that speak a Turkic language.

Kurds

The Kurds are the largest ethnic minority in Turkey today. They make up an estimated 17 percent of the population. Although most Turkish Kurds have traditionally lived in southeastern Anatolia, they have an increasing presence in urban areas.

Tensions have existed between the Kurds and the Turkish government since Turkey's founding in 1923. In a treaty signed after World War I, the Kurds were promised that their homeland—Kurdistan—would become an independent state. Instead, it was divided among the newly created states of Turkey, Iran, Iraq, and Syria. The Kurds in Turkey launched several armed uprisings against the new government in an effort to establish a

Kurdish people, proud of their heritage, are hopeful that reforms of the last decade will continue to promote their rights and increase their political voice in Turkey.

separate state. These rebellions were crushed by the new government, setting the stage for tensions that continue today.

Many of the reforms implemented by the republic's government were intended to erase ethnic differences in order to mold a Turkish identity. As one of the few non-Turkic groups, the Kurds were particularly affected by new policies that prohibited languages other than Turkish to be taught in school or spoken in public. In an effort to contain the Kurdish rebellions and prevent any others from occurring, the new government also banned Kurdish political parties.

In 1986 the Kurdistan Workers Party (Turkish acronym PKK) began organizing guerrilla attacks against the Turkish military forces in southeastern Anatolia. (*Guerrillas* are armed fighters who are trying to overthrow their government.) Their goal was the creation of a separate Kurdish state.

The violent guerrilla war between Turkey and the Kurds continued for more than a decade. In 1988, across the border in Iraq, Saddam Hussein, who was also fighting Kurdish rebels in his own country, launched biochemical attacks on Kurdish villages. Thousands of Iraqi Kurds sought refuge in Turkey, but Turkey and Iraq had a standing agreement to allow each other to follow Kurdish rebels across their shared border. Attacks against

THE TURKISH LANGUAGE

Turkey's official language is Turkish, a language that belongs to the Altaic-Uralic family of languages that originated in central and northern Asia. (Arabic, the predominant language in the Middle East, belongs to the Semitic language family, while Persian, like English, belongs to the Indo-European language family.) When central Asian Turks converted to Islam in the tenth century, the Turkish language was heavily influenced by Arabic and Persian. Scholars employed Arabic script for written Turkish during this period. During the Ottoman era, a palace form of the language called Ottoman Turkish developed, which incorporated many Arabic and Persian words.

Language reform became a major goal of the new Republic of Turkey in the 1920s. The Latin alphabet (used by Western languages, including English) was modified to fit the Turkish vowel system and has been used for written Turkish since 1928. This change was implemented to make it easier for citizens to become literate and also to emphasize the desire of the Turkish government to identify the new country with Europe rather than the Middle East. Each letter used in Turkish has a specific sound, and every letter is pronounced, making it a relatively easy language to learn. As part of the language reform, numerous Arabic and Persian words were purged from the vocabulary. Today, about 80 percent of the Turkish language is based on authentic Turkish words, about double the number in the early years of the republic.

Did You Know?

About half of all Kurds live in Turkey. Nearly all of the rest live in Iran, Iraq, and Syria.

Kurdish rebels in each other's country were also authorized. After the Persian Gulf War, when the Iraqi Kurds gained worldwide sympathy for their treatment at the hands of Saddam Hussein, people in other countries became more aware of Turkey's oppression of the Kurds also.

The Kurds finally signed a truce with Turkey's government in 2001. There are still high levels of suspicion on the part of both groups, however. Recognizing the need for greater unity, the Turkish parliament recently passed laws easing the restrictions against use of the Kurdish language.

Other Ethnic Groups

In the late nineteenth century, Greeks and Armenians made up about 30 percent of the population in Thrace and Anatolia. However, increasing

His Holiness Karekin I, Catholicos of All Armenians. Despite brutal persecution by the Ottomans during World War I, the strong religious beliefs of the Armenians who have remained in Turkey encourage peaceful coexistence for all ethnicities within the country.

ethnic tensions and several forced resettlements resulted in a steep decline in the number of Greeks and Armenians living in Turkey today. In 1939, France—which ruled Syria after World War I (1914–1918)—transferred the area of Hatay, also known as Alexandretta, in northwestern Syria to Turkey. This instantly increased the size of Turkey's Arab population. Other small ethnic groups also live in Turkey today, although most describe themselves as Turks.

Arabs

Arabs, most of whom live in the Arab Platform region bordering Syria, make up less than 2 percent of Turkey's population. This makes them the third largest ethnic group in Turkey.

The Laz

The Laz are non-Turkic Muslims who live in the eastern Black Sea region. They are descendants of Muslims who came to Anatolia from the Caucasus region centuries ago. Their skill in boatbuilding and navigating the often rough waters of the Black Sea is well-known in the region. Although most followed Christian traditions while under Byzantine rule, today the majority are Muslims.

Armenians

Before World War I, 1.5 to 2 million Armenians lived in Anatolia, most in the eastern provinces. In 1915, the Ottoman government forced all Armenians out of eastern Anatolia, claiming that they were collaborating with the Russian army. (In World War I, the Ottomans, Germany, and other Axis powers fought against Britain, France, Russia, the United States, and other Allied powers.)

THE HEMSINLIS

A small community of Armenians known as the Hemsinlis (HEM-shin-lees) have lived in the eastern Black Sea region since the Byzantine era. During the Ottoman period, they converted from Christianity to Islam and began following Turkish customs. As a result, they escaped the mass deportations that took place during and immediately after World War I.

The Hemsinlis are known for their skill in cooking, especially desserts. Some of the best-known pastry shops in Turkish cities are run by Hemsinlis.

Today, the Armenian community in Turkey numbers 40,000. Most Turkish Armenians have professional or business careers and live in the Istanbul area. Newspapers, churches, and schools help the community maintain its Armenian identity.

Greeks

In the years during and after World War I, Allied countries jockeyed to gain control of regions of the former Ottoman Empire that would protect or advance their interests. According to agreements negotiated during the war, Russia, France, Italy, and Greece were supportive of an independent Armenia and Kurdistan, but would be awarded portions of Anatolia and Thrace. Before the territory could be divided up, however, the Turkish War of Independence broke out, and Turkish forces prohibited the European countries from taking control.

In 1919, Greek forces invading western Anatolia were met by armies of Turkish *nationalists,* who wanted Turkey to become an independent nation. During the ensuing three years of war, many Greeks living in Thrace and Anatolia fled to Greece. The Greeks were eventually defeated in 1922, and as part of the truce, about 2 million Greeks were forced to leave Anatolia in 1924. Only 200,000 were permitted to stay.

In the 1930s, the Turkish government again began encouraging Greeks to leave the country. Many did so, and today the Greek community in Turkey numbers less than 20,000. Most live in Istanbul or on two islands near the Dardanelles. The majority belong to the Orthodox Christian Church.

Jews

Turkey has never had a large Jewish population; in the early twentieth century, about 90,000 Jews lived there. In 1948, about one-third of the Jewish community emigrated to Israel. Over the following decades, thousands more followed. In 1995, about 20,000 Jews remained in Turkey. Most are Sephardic (suh-FAR-dik) Jews, descendants of Jews who were forced out of Spain during the fifteenth century. They speak Ladino, which is a form of Spanish. The rest of the Jewish community is descended from the Ashkenazi—Eastern European Jews whose native language is Yiddish. Most Jews living in Turkey today speak Turkish and own small businesses.

Land and Resources

Turkey's land and climate are quite diverse, with an amazing richness of plant and animal life.

Geography

Turkey, the fourth largest country in the Middle East, stretches over 301,384 square miles (780,580 square kilometers), making it slightly larger than Texas. Most of the country—about 97 percent—lies in Asia and is known as Anatolia, while Thrace—the region that lies in Europe—makes up the remaining 3 percent. The Black Sea forms Turkey's northern border. Georgia, Armenia, Azerbaijan, and Iran share Turkey's eastern border, while Iraq, Syria, and the Mediterranean Sea lie to the south. Bulgaria, Greece, and the Aegean Sea border Turkey on the west.

Turkey can be divided into seven geographical regions. Three of these are coastal regions: the Black Sea region, the Aegean region, and the Mediterranean region. Three more regions lie within the Anatolian interior: the Northern Anatolian and Taurus mountain ranges, the Anatolian Plateau, and the Eastern Highlands. The seventh region—the Arabian Platform—lies near the Syrian border in southeastern Turkey.

Fishing, an important industry in the Black Sea coastal towns, is threatened by pollution and damage to the Black Sea ecosystem.

The Black Sea Region

The Black Sea region stretches the length of Turkey's northern shore, from Bulgaria to Georgia. Although it is Turkey's northernmost region, the narrow coastal plain boasts a warm, temperate climate with plenty of rainfall. Rising behind the coastal plain is a nearly solid wall of mountains that, throughout history, has cut off the Black Sea coastal villages from the rest of Anatolia. The highest peaks are in the east, reaching 9,800 to 13,100 feet high (3,000 to 4,000 meters). Several rivers flow down from the mountains to the coastal plain.

Commercial agriculture is the major economic activity in the Black Sea region; tobacco, citrus fruits, hazelnuts, and tea are the most profitable crops. Coal is mined in the western Black Sea region, and many heavy industries are located there as well. Fishing is also important to the local economy.

The Aegean Region

The Aegean region includes Thrace as well as the coastal plains of Anatolia. It is the most densely populated region in Turkey, home to some of Turkey's largest cities, including Istanbul and Izmir, a major

The Bosporus Bridge straddles one of the world's most beautiful and busiest ports.

manufacturing center. Thrace and Anatolia are separated by the Bosporus, the Sea of Marmara (MAR-muh-ruh), and the Dardanelles Strait. (The Bosporus is a short strait that connects the Black Sea and the Sea of Marmara, while the Dardanelles Strait connects the Sea of Marmara with the Aegean Sea.)

Thrace features gently rolling hills in the west, building into mountains in the east. Much of this land is suitable for farming. The Aegean coastal plains of Anatolia are narrow, but farming is widespread here as well, given the fertile soil and warm climate of the region. Citrus and other fruits, grains, and cotton are the biggest crops in the Aegean region. The beaches that line the Aegean coast draw thousands of tourists each year.

The Mediterranean Region

The coastal plains of the Mediterranean region are quite narrow. The Taurus Mountains climb sharply, reaching elevations of 6,560 to 9,000 feet (2,000 to 2,750 meters) and separating the Mediterranean region from the Anatolian interior. Here, as in the Aegean region, the fertile soil and warm climate accommodate intensive farming. Cotton is the most significant crop, although fruits, vegetables, and grains are also grown. The tourist industry is well established here as well, with sandy beaches the prime attraction.

The Northern Anatolian and Taurus Mountains

Two long mountain ranges—the Northern Anatolian Mountains in the north and the Taurus Mountains in the south—have isolated the Black Sea and Mediterranean regions from the rest of Turkey for centuries. Running parallel to the Black Sea coast, the Northern Anatolian Mountains (sometimes called the Pontus or Pontic Mountains) divide the Black Sea region from the Anatolian Plateau. The western end of the range is relatively low, with most peaks below 5,000 feet (1,500 meters). Eastward, the mountains get taller, reaching elevations greater than 10,000 feet (3,000 meters). Because the northern slopes receive plenty of rainfall, they are often heavily wooded. The drier southern slopes have few trees, however. Several rivers flow down the northern slopes and empty into the Black Sea.

The Taurus range runs just north of the Mediterranean region, with few passes through its craggy length. The Taurus Mountains are very tall, rising over 10,000 feet (3,000 meters). Since ancient times, small flames have appeared to dance across the rocky face of the mountains. This phenomenon, called the Chimera (kigh-MEAR-uh) after the fire-breathing she-monster in Greek mythology, occurs when gases such as methane escape from the rocks and burn naturally.

The Anatolian Plateau

The Northern Anatolian and Taurus mountain ranges frame the Anatolian Plateau, which extends from the Aegean coastal plain eastward to the point where the two ranges meet. The plateau, with its arid grasslands and rugged terrain, is considered the heart of the country. Turkey's capital city—Ankara (ANG-kuh-ruh)—is located in this region. Most people living in the Anatolian Plateau region raise crops such as wheat, barley, corn, cotton, and fruits. Opium poppies and tobacco are also big moneymaking crops. In some parts of the plateau, enough rain falls to support the crops, but irrigation is necessary in other areas. The southern section of the plateau has several lakes. These lakes are quite salty and often flood.

The Eastern Highlands

The Eastern Highlands (also known as the Anti-Taurus because they are located opposite the Taurus range) begin at the point where the Taurus and Northern Anatolian Mountains meet and extend to Turkey's eastern border. This rugged, mountainous region has an average elevation of more than 10,000 feet (3,000 meters). Turkey's largest lake, Lake Van, lies in the Eastern Highlands, as does the highest peak—Mount Ararat, which rises to 16,949 feet (5,166 meters). Many rivers and streams cut through the region, including two rivers—the Tigris and Euphrates—that supported some of the world's earliest civilizations. Much of the historical region of Kurdistan lies within the Eastern Highlands.

Did You Know?

According to the Old Testament of the Bible, Noah's ark came to rest on Mount Ararat as the floodwaters receded. No scientific evidence has been found to support this claim.

The Arabian Platform

Near the Syrian border lies the Arabian Platform, a region once known as Upper Mesopotamia. This barren plateau is bracketed by the Tigris and Euphrates rivers. Agriculture is possible near the rivers, but this region remains the poorest and least populated in Turkey. Several dams have been built on the Tigris and Euphrates rivers, providing much-needed water throughout the region.

Major Cities

Just three decades ago, over half of Turkey's population lived in rural areas. Today, about two-thirds live in Turkey's growing urban areas. Social classes have developed along with the urbanization, diminishing the regional differences that once distinguished the various groups of ethnic Turks. Generally speaking, power—both in politics and business—and education determine one's social standing. The upper class typically includes government officials, professionals, and wealthy business owners. Members of the middle class work in many different professions, but nearly all have a college degree. The fastest growing population in Turkey's cities is the lower class, estimated at 60 percent in most cities. Primarily rural villagers who have migrated to the cities looking for work since the 1950s, they often live in *gecekondus* (GEDJ-eh-KOHN-doos)—slums consisting of temporary shelters that became permanent. While some *gecekondus* have access to electricity and water services, most do not.

Ankara

The capital city of Turkey since the republic was established in 1923, Ankara shares many similarities with other modern cities. Glass and concrete buildings reach for the sky in Ankara's government and business districts. Universities draw thousands of students, while the city's industrial base attracts people looking for work. Sprawling suburbs surround the city.

Like many places in Turkey, Ankara has its roots in antiquity. It was established at the junction of two important trade routes during the Hittite period, over 3,000 years ago. Under Ottoman rule, the city was known as Angora, a reference to the type of goats that were raised there. (Angora goats produce a fine wool known as *mohair*.)

In 1920, Kemal Ataturk—Turkey's founding father—selected Angora as the capital of the new republic and changed its name to Ankara as part of the movement to purge the new republic of non-Turkish words. The city was modeled after European cities, with wide streets and parks, but its booming growth has obscured that design in many places.

Many of the nearly 5 million residents of Ankara live in the *gecekondus* that surround the city. All residents, rich and poor, had to deal for years with terrible air pollution, especially during the winter months when coal was burned to heat homes and businesses. The level of pollution has been reduced dramatically in recent years.

Even Turkey's most modern cities boast architectural antiquities that remind residents and visitors alike of the country's long, proud history.

Istanbul

Istanbul is an ancient city that served as the center of several different empires. Around the middle of the seventh century B.C.E., the city was founded as Byzantium. Alexander the Great conquered the city in the fourth century B.C.E., and it later became part of the Roman Empire. When Roman emperor Constantine took the city as his eastern capital in the fourth century C.E., he renamed it Constantinople. The growing city stood as the capital of the Byzantine Empire until the Ottomans captured it in 1453. Under Ottoman rule, the city became known as Istanbul. It remained the administrative center of the Ottoman Empire until the empire was dismantled after World War I.

Although it is no longer a capital, Istanbul remains the largest city in Turkey. The Bosporus divides Istanbul into European and Asian sections, making it the only city in the world to be built on two continents. Suspended bridges and ferries connect the two parts of the city.

Many buildings from the Byzantine and Ottoman eras still stand in Old Istanbul (on the European side of the city). The Hagia Sophia, or Church of the Divine Wisdom, was commissioned by the Byzantine emperor Justinian I as a Christian Orthodox basilica in the sixth century. Inside, its soaring domes are covered with millions of gold mosaic tiles. Under the Ottomans, the church was converted to a mosque. In the early years of the republic, the Hagia Sophia (also known as the Aya Sophia) was made into a museum.

The Topkapi Palace is another favorite tourist site in Old Istanbul. The palace was both home to the Ottoman sultans and the main seat of the imperial government from 1465 until the mid-nineteenth century. The royal family's living quarters alone include hundreds of opulent rooms.

In the seventeenth century, Sultan Ahmet I ordered the construction of a mosque that would surpass the glories of the Hagia Sophia. The Blue Mosque, named for the blue tiles that decorate the interior, was the result. The mosque is topped by a series of domes and minarets that are designed to draw the worshipers' eyes toward heaven.

Although Istanbul has a long and storied past, it also plays an important role in modern Turkey. Revitalized in the 1980s and 1990s as a tourist destination, it is also an important industrial city. Its population is growing rapidly as rural Turks, unable to find work in the countryside, migrate to the urban areas. Today the population stands at 14 million, compared with 1.5 million in 1950. Many of these new urbanites live in poverty in the *gecekondus* that surround the city. Traffic snarls and pollution are growing problems.

Climate

The Black Sea region is the wettest region in Turkey because of the mountains that rise from the coastal plain. As the moisture-laden air rises to cross the mountains, it cools and the moisture falls as rain. Rain falls in the eastern coastal region year-round, averaging 55 inches (140 centimeters) annually. The Black Sea region has warm summers and mild winters.

The Aegean and Mediterranean regions both enjoy a typical Mediterranean climate—cool, wet winters followed by long, warm summers. Average temperatures range from 37° to 48° F (3° to 9° C) in January, while July temperatures rarely rise above 83° F (28° C). Rainfall totals vary from 23 to 51 inches (58 to 130 centimeters) each year, with the western coasts receiving more rain than those in the east. Most of the rain falls during the winter months.

Surrounded by mountains, the Anatolian Plateau gets little moisture. Rainfall averages 16 inches (40 centimeters) per year, with most of that falling in the higher elevations during the winter months. Winters are harsh, with temperatures hovering around freezing most of the time. The eastern plateau has several mountainous areas that have recorded temperatures as low as –40° F (–40° C). Summers reach the other extreme, with little rainfall and temperatures regularly rising above 86° F (30° C).

The climate in the Eastern Highlands region can be forbidding. Summers are hot with very little rainfall, while heavy snows and extremely low temperatures are common in the winter. Winter storms often leave whole villages stranded for days at a time.

Natural Resources

Turkey has several small deposits of important minerals, among them chromium, bauxite, and copper. The metals that are mined in Turkey are used in the production of iron and steel, aluminum, fertilizers, and cement. Some minerals, such as boron, are exported.

Although Turkey has coal, natural gas, and oil deposits, they are not extensive enough to meet Turkey's energy demands. As a result, Turkey uses its water resources to produce electricity as well as for agricultural irrigation. The ambitious Southeast Anatolia Project (Turkish acronym GAP), first announced in 1977, outlined plans for twenty-two dams and

TURKEY'S METALS

Various metals are mined in Turkey. They are used in many industries, both in Turkey and internationally.

Antimony	Used in Biblical times as a cosmetic and medicine; today's most important application is in storage batteries and as a flame-retardant for children's clothing and industrial fabrics.
Asbestos	Fire-resistant asbestos was once widely used in residential and industrial materials, including floor and ceiling tiles, insulating cement, and pipe coverings. Asbestos breaks down over time; inhaling the dust makes individuals more likely to develop cancer. Today, the primary application for asbestos is in the production of roofing materials and gaskets.
Bauxite	Used in the production of aluminum.
Boron	Used widely in detergents and as an insect repellent. Industrial applications include the production of enamels for household appliances. Turkey and the United States are the world's largest producers of boron.
Chromium	Used in combination with other metals to increase hardness and reduce corrosion; today's most important application is in the production of stainless steel.
Copper	One of the first metals used by humans. Today, its primary use is electrical, including wiring, telecommunications, and the production of electrical and electronic products.
Lead	Used for at least 5,000 years, its early uses included building materials, ceramic glazes, and water pipes. Today, lead is used primarily in storage batteries and ammunition.
Magnetite	A common form of iron ore; primary use is in the production of iron and steel.
Mercury	Once commonly found in thermometers its primary application today is industrial chemicals and electronics.
Silver	Used throughout history for jewelry, trade, and as a basis for monetary systems. Today, industrial applications include mirrors, electronics, and photography.
Sulfur	Used primarily in the form of sulfuric acid, a critical material in many industrial processes and fertilizer production.
Zinc	One of the most widely used metals in the world. Used mainly as a corrosion-resistant coating (as in galvanized metals) and in the production of bronze and brass. Also used in rubber, chemical, paint, and agricultural industries.

nineteen hydroelectric plants that were built on the Tigris and
Euphrates rivers in the 1980s and 1990s. The Ataturk Dam, completed
in 1990, is the ninth largest rock-filled dam in the world. Its
hydroelectric plant generates almost 9 billion kilowatt hours of
electricity each year, about 8 percent of Turkey's annual electricity
consumption. (As a comparison, a typical U.S. household uses 10,000
kilowatt hours of electricity annually. This means that the energy
produced by Ataturk Dam's hydroelectric plant could power all of the
households in Utah and Wyoming for one year.)

After the water passes through the hydroelectric plant, it flows
through concrete-lined tunnels 25 feet (7.6 meters) in diameter. The
tunnels direct the water to irrigation networks in southeastern Turkey.
This project, combined with other GAP efforts, will double the amount
of land that can be farmed. Each farm will also be able to plant and
harvest two to three crops each year. Already, the improvements that
have resulted from the Ataturk Dam have raised incomes and the
standard of living in this poor area.

WHOSE WATER IS IT?

The Tigris and Euphrates rivers that
originate in Turkey wander across Syria and
Iraq until they merge and become the Shatt
al-Arab, which flows into the Persian Gulf.
These two rivers fed the plains of ancient
Mesopotamia, enabling the development of
some of the world's first civilizations. Today,
the water they carry is equally important to
the people in these three arid countries, for
drinking water, agricultural irrigation, and
the generation of hydroelectricity.

Because the water carried in the rivers is
fundamental to life in the regions they flow
through, anything that threatens the flow of
water—such as a dam—has the potential of
causing an international problem. When
Syria built dams on the Euphrates in the
1960s and 1970s, Iraq protested
vehemently, claiming that millions of Iraqi
farmers no longer had enough water to
grow crops. In 1977, Turkey announced the

Southeast Anatolia Project (Turkish
acronym GAP), a plan to complete several
major projects—including twenty-two dams
and nineteen hydroelectric plants—on the
Tigris and Euphrates. Syria and Iraq
immediately objected to the plan, saying
that they stood to lose 70 percent of the
water they needed if the dams were built.

Turkey is forging ahead with GAP
projects, arguing that because the Tigris
and Euphrates originate in Turkey, the water
belongs to Turkey. Syria and Iraq argue that
the rivers are international and that the
water should be divided according to each
country's needs. Iraq also points out that
the two rivers have irrigated Iraqi fields
since Mesopotamian days. It views the
water from the rivers as its historical right.

With no resolution in sight, the question
remains: Who will control the water in the
Tigris and Euphrates?

Plants and Animals

Turkey's varying geography and climate have fostered a rich diversity of plants and animals. Its location at the junction of Europe and Asia has also contributed to the number of species that can be found within its borders. Many of its animal species first appeared in present-day Turkey during the Ice Age, when animals migrated southward looking for warmer climates. Many plant species also date back to antiquity.

Turkey is widely known as a gene center for many cultivated crops. This means that the ancestors of plants such as wheat and apricots still grow wild in Turkey. Biotechnology innovations allow scientists to select genes from the ancestral plants, such as the genes that increase resistance to disease, and use them to improve today's crops.

The sheer number of plant species found in Turkey is amazing. There are over 9,000 species of wildflowers alone. Many ornamental flowers—including tulips, lilies, and crocuses—were originally

Turkey's diverse geography supports many agricultural industries. The southeast region is ideal for farming and raising livestock.

cultivated from Turkish wildflowers. Many plants used for food, including barley, chickpeas, lentils, figs, cherries, and several nuts, are native to Turkey. Olives, grapes, kiwis, bananas, and avocados are grown commercially, as are cotton and tobacco. Crops that require more water—such as tea, flax, hazelnuts, and plums—are grown in the Black Sea region.

Forests of pine, fir, and cedar grow throughout the coastal and mountain regions of Turkey. The red pine forests found in the coastal regions are well adapted to the hot, dry summers, while cedar and fir are found at higher elevations. The north slopes of the Northern Anatolian Mountains are thick with hardwood and evergreen forests. Beech, oak, and maple benefit from abundant rainfall in that region, as do several pine and spruce species.

In contrast, the Anatolian Plateau, Eastern Highlands, and Arabian Platform have few trees. Although grasses and flowers are common in the western and central plateau, the land becomes increasingly barren in the east and southeast.

Turkey's diverse regions support a wide variety of animal species as well. Over 80,000 species have been identified in Turkey—more than one and a half times as many species as are found in the entire continent of Europe. The pheasant, the domestic sheep, and the fallow deer all originated in Turkey. Big cats, including lions and tigers, were once common in the Anatolian Plateau. Today, most of Turkey's wildlife is found in the mountain regions and in the many national parks that have been established to protect native species. Brown bears, lynx, wolves, wild boars, water buffalo, and even leopards can be seen in the wild in these areas. Hundreds of species of birds live in or migrate through Turkey, supported by the many wetlands. Among them are flamingos, ducks, geese, herons, and endangered species such as the Dalmatian pelican and the pygmy cormorant.

The coastal waters of the Aegean and Mediterranean provide habitats for an equally diverse sea life. Several endangered species, including the monk seal and the loggerhead turtle, are found off the coast of Turkey. The Turkish government is committed to protecting these species. Several beaches and bays have been closed to tourism in an effort to protect sea turtle nesting grounds. Freshwater plants and animals once thrived in the Black Sea, but pollution and increasing salinity have caused a sharp decline in marine life in this area.

History

Ancient Anatolia

Long before the Central Turks arrived in Anatolia, Stone Age people were making their mark in the region. Archaeologists have excavated one of the oldest cities in the world near Konya, in central Turkey. Artifacts discovered there date back to 6500 B.C.E. Thousands of years later, around 2500 B.C.E., the discovery of copper and the development of techniques to work with it transformed the region.

Assyrian merchants from Mesopotamia (in present-day Iraq) colonized areas of Anatolia between 2500 and 2000 B.C.E. From these settlements, they helped the Mesopotamian empires obtain the copper (and later bronze and iron) they needed for weapons. By 1500 B.C.E., rich deposits of iron ore had been discovered in southern Anatolia. Iron works were soon established, and the region became known as an iron production center.

Early Empires

Around 1700 B.C.E., hordes of warriors from Asia crossed the Caucasus Mountains and streamed into Anatolia. After conquering the people living there, they adopted much of the native culture, including the cuneiform alphabet that was in use and the gods that were worshiped. (A *cuneiform* alphabet uses wedge-shaped characters.)

The Hittite Empire, which included eastern Anatolia and northern Syria, became known as a trading center as well as a political center.

THE LOST CITY OF TROY

One of the most enduring stories in Greek literature is the tale of Greek heroes outwitting the citizens of Troy through the use of a wooden horse. In the story, Helen, the most beautiful woman in the world and the Queen of Sparta, is kidnapped and taken to Troy. Achilles and Odysseus are among the Greek heroes who accompany Helen's husband, Menelaus, to Troy, where they battle the Trojans for ten years but cannot get past the city walls. Odysseus proposes building a huge wooden horse.

The Greek heroes hide inside the horse, and the Trojans unwittingly pull their enemies into the city. In the ensuing battle, the Greeks are victorious. For centuries, people believed that the city of Troy was fictional. But in 1871, German archaeologist Heinrich Schliemann discovered the ruins of the actual city of Troy in northwest Anatolia. It was built upon the ruins of cities dating back to 3600 B.C.E., and other cities had been built atop Troy.

IMPORTANT EVENTS IN TURKEY'S HISTORY

6500 B.C.E. Stone Age people settle near Konya in present-day Turkey.

2500 B.C.E. The discovery of copper transforms life in Anatolia.

1500 B.C.E. Anatolia gains recognition as a center for iron production.

546 B.C.E. Cyrus the Great leads the Persian army into Anatolia and defeats the city-states there.

333 B.C.E. Alexander the Great crushes the Persians in Anatolia.

43 C.E. Anatolia becomes part of the Roman Empire.

285 The Roman emperor splits the empire into Latin- and Greek-speaking regions.

330 Roman emperor Constantine the Great establishes his capital in Byzantium, renaming it Constantinople (present-day Istanbul).

1284 Osman I becomes the first ruler of what will develop into the Ottoman Empire.

1453 Mehmet II defeats the Byzantines to gain control of Constantinople, which he renames Istanbul.

1860s The Young Ottomans press for changes in government, including a constitution and an elected parliament.

1907 Reformers organize the Committee of Union and Progress and become known as the Young Turks.

1908 The armed forces revolt, forcing the sultan to schedule parliamentary elections. The Young Turks win most seats.

1913 Enver Pasha organizes a coup against the liberal Young Turk government and institutes a dictatorship.

1914 The Ottomans sign an alliance to fight with Germany in World War I.

1915 The Ottomans force 1.5 million Armenians to leave their homes in eastern Anatolia.

1918 The Allied Powers defeat the Axis forces and begin to dismantle the Ottoman Empire.

1919 Mustafa Kemal argues for the creation of a Turkish state. Greece invades Anatolia.

1920 Turkish nationalists organize a Grand National Assembly and elect Kemal as their president.

1923 The Treaty of Lausanne establishes an independent Turkish republic.

1939 World War II begins, and Turkey remains neutral until 1945 when it declares war on Germany.

1945 Turkey becomes one of the founding members of the United Nations (UN).

1950 The Democrat Party (DP) becomes the second political party to be established in Turkey.

1960 The government imposes martial law throughout Turkey following increasing violence between political parties.

1961 The military gives up control of the government following the establishment of a new constitution and an election.

1971 Violence increases throughout Turkey.

1980 The Turkish military takes control of the Turkish government once again.

1982 Voters approve a new constitution, marking the beginning of the Third Republic of Turkey.

1991 Iraq invades Kuwait, triggering the Persian Gulf War. Turkey sends troops to fight as part of the international coalition.

mid-1990s Islamic fundamentalists gain strength in Turkish politics.

2000 Voters elect Ahmet Necdet Sezer president of Turkey.

2002 The Islamist Justice and Development Party gains power in the Turkish parliament. Recep Tayyip Erdogan is named prime minister.

The Hittites kept written records of their exploits, and a written *constitution* guided the rulers. Although the Hittites had a professional army, they reserved war to be used as a final resort. The Hittite Empire remained powerful until 1200 B.C.E., when it fell to invaders known as the Sea Peoples.

Several centuries of turmoil followed the collapse of the Hittite Empire as small kingdoms vied for power. The Phrygians emerged as leaders of an empire that encompassed much of central and western Anatolia. They followed the same pattern as the Hittites had before them, adopting the Hittite culture and political structure as their own. The Phrygians remained in power until the seventh century B.C.E., when the Cimmerians—nomads from Asia—defeated them.

About the time that the Cimmerians were conquering the Phrygians, a city-state known as Lydia came to power in western Anatolia. The Lydians were known for their gold and immense wealth. One Lydian king, Croesus, gained a reputation as the richest man in the world.

The Greeks

Centuries before the Lydians came to power in western Anatolia, Greek traders were in contact with people living along the Aegean coast. By the beginning of the ninth century B.C.E., colonies of Greek settlers had been established in several commercial centers along the Aegean coast, including Troy, Ephesus, and Miletus. When the Lydians came to power in the region, the Greeks were allowed to maintain their own political and social structure. In return, they had to pay taxes to the Lydians.

When the Persian army first appeared in western Anatolia, the Greeks welcomed them. After years of Persian rule, however, the Greeks living in Anatolia asked Macedonia for help in overthrowing the Persian Empire. In 333 B.C.E., the Macedonian emperor, Alexander the Great, led his army against the Persians in Anatolia. After the Persians were crushed, Anatolia was added to the Macedonian Empire.

When Alexander died ten years later, his empire was divided up among his generals. Seleucus Nicator claimed the section that included southern and western Anatolia, Thrace, Syria, Mesopotamia, and Persia. Seleucus and his descendants—the Seleucid Dynasty—ruled over this region until 64 B.C.E. During this time, many Greek colonists settled in the region, facilitating the spread of Greek language and culture.

The Romans

The Roman Empire invaded Anatolia in the second century B.C.E. By 43 C.E., Rome controlled all of Anatolia. With the strength of the Roman Empire behind it, Anatolia flourished. Secure from invasions, many provinces became wealthy through trade with other parts of the empire.

In 285, the Roman Empire was split into two administrative regions to make it easier to rule. The eastern empire included provinces that spoke Greek, while the western empire governed the Latin-speaking provinces. When Constantine the Great became emperor in 330, he established his eastern capital in the city of Byzantium and renamed it Constantinople (present-day Istanbul).

Christianity had been introduced in Anatolia soon after the death of Jesus Christ. It had spread throughout much of the eastern empire by the end of the third century. By the end of the fourth century, Constantinople had become the center of the Greek Church. The Hagia Sophia, or Church of Divine Wisdom, was built in the middle of the sixth century as an inspiration to Christians.

Rome and the western provinces of the empire fell to the Goths late in the fifth century. Following this disaster, the eastern empire became known as the Byzantine Empire. It remained strong and even expanded. When Muslim conquerors rode north out of Arabia in the seventh century, the Byzantine Empire included Greece, Anatolia, Syria, Egypt, Sicily, most of Italy, the Balkans, and several North African regions.

The Seljuk Turks

Beginning in the sixth century and continuing over the course of several centuries, Turks from central Asia began migrating to the west. One group—the Oguz, also known as the Seljuks after their chief—arrived in Baghdad (center of the Islamic world) in the tenth century. As Muslims and warriors, the Seljuks offered their services to the Abbasids, who were in control of the Islamic empire.

The Seljuks were assigned to guard the frontiers of the empire. In 1055, however, a Seljuk chief named Tugrul Bey led his army into Baghdad and overthrew the Abbasids. Although he did not claim the title of *caliph* (religious leader of Islam), Tugrul Bey did take the title of *sultan,* indicating that he was the supreme ruler of Persia and Mesopotamia.

Soon the Seljuks' attention was drawn northward. They began launching attacks in Anatolia in the late eleventh century and, in 1071, defeated the Byzantine army in eastern Anatolia. The region was divided into sultanates (small states), the most important of which was Rum (referring to Rome). The Byzantine Empire remained strong in western Anatolia and along the northern and southern coasts.

As the Turks settled in Anatolia, they established trade routes between their new home and other Middle Eastern countries. Along the trade routes, they built *caravansaries,* or rest stops, similar to inns.

Along with the Turks came Islam. The empire that had remained predominantly Christian for over seven centuries was now under attack by Muslim armies. Christian leaders in Constantinople and Rome spoke out against this threat to Christian lands. In 1095, Pope Urban II issued a call for European warriors to travel to the Holy Land (Palestine) and win it back, thus beginning the Crusades.

Seljuk control of Anatolia ended in 1258, when the Mongols invaded western Asia.

One column and some foundation stones are all that remain of the Artemision in Selcuk, a temple built in the sixth century B.C. and renovated in 334 and 250 B.C. In the background is Ephesus, home to a museum that displays findings from the excavations in surrounding areas.

The Rise of the Ottoman Empire

In the late thirteenth century, a tribe related to the Seljuks was granted territory in northwestern Anatolia, provided its warriors could seize the land from the Byzantines. Their efforts were successful, and around 1284, control of the territory passed to Osman I. Osman I was ambitious and set out to increase his holdings by attacking lands to the west. He was supported by Turkish, Arab, and Iranian mercenaries who were drawn by the opportunity to share in the plunder from the newly captured lands. As his empire grew, it became known as the Osmanli, or Ottoman, Empire.

Osman I was the first leader and visionary of the powerful, long-ruling Ottoman Empire.

The Ottomans saw their success in capturing new lands as a sign that God wanted them to create and rule over an Islamic empire. The sultans (rulers) took the title of caliph and claimed spiritual leadership of the Islamic world as well as of their empire. Islam was integrated into all aspects of government and daily life.

The early strategy of the Ottomans was to conquer lands to the west, which were not controlled by Muslims, by force. Muslim-controlled lands to the east were often added to the empire through intermarriage, although some were purchased from the Turkmans who controlled much of that territory. By the end of the fourteenth century, the Ottomans controlled much of the Balkan Peninsula as well as most of western Anatolia. Constantinople, however, remained firmly under control of the Byzantines.

The Mongols, led by Timur (known in the West as Tamerlane), gained a foothold in Anatolia in 1402. Within two decades, however, the Ottomans had forced the Mongols from the region. With the Mongols gone, the Ottoman sultan Mehmet II turned his attention toward Constantinople. His forces laid siege to the city in 1453, and after fifty days, Constantinople finally fell into Ottoman hands. After this victory, which symbolized the growing power of the empire, Mehmet II named the city Istanbul and made it the imperial city. Cathedrals and churches, including the Hagia Sophia, were converted to mosques. Although Istanbul was now the center of Sunni Islam, it remained an important

Did You Know?

The Ottoman Empire, one of the most powerful empires in world history, ruled for six centuries. At its height, it controlled territories in North Africa, the Middle East, and Eastern Europe.

OTTOMAN HIERARCHY

The Ottomans established a new social structure in their empire. The ruler was known as the sultan. He had the final authority in all areas—political, military, judicial, social, and religious. Theoretically, the sultan answered only to God. However, he had to keep a large constituency happy, including the military and religious leaders.

The ruling class was the aristocracy, loyal to the sultan and serving him in various roles. In the early Ottoman period, the ruling class was predominantly Muslim, but in later years, Greeks, Armenians, and Jews were appointed to diplomatic and other official posts.

The sultan was advised by a council of ministers known as the *divan*. The chief minister, who held a great deal of power, was called the grand *vizier* (vuh-ZEAR). The entrance to the building that housed the divan was called the Bab-i Ali, the High Gate or Sublime Porte. Over time, the Ottoman government became known simply as the Porte. High-ranking officials who governed the provinces were called pashas.

Christian center as well, with the patriarch of the Greek Orthodox Church maintaining the church headquarters in Istanbul.

In the early sixteenth century, Sultan Selim I led military campaigns in Syria, Palestine, and Egypt and added those lands to the empire. Despite the empire's growing size, it didn't become a world power until Selim I's son—Suleyman (SOO-lay-mon) the Magnificent—assumed the throne in 1520.

Under Suleyman, the Ottoman Empire reached its peak, stretching from Budapest (in present-day Hungary) to North Africa and including parts of Arabia, western Asia, and all of Anatolia. Known as the "Lawgiver," Suleyman formalized social and governmental institutions into law. These laws divided society into the ruling and subject classes and allowed the sultan to take advantage of the empire's wealth.

The members of the ruling class were assigned to one of four areas. Those in the Imperial Institution worked within the palace, serving the sultan. The Military Institution, which included the Janissary Corps and the cavalry, kept order in the empire. Members of the Scribal Institution assessed and collected taxes, while the Religious and Cultural Institution supervised Islamic practices as well as the education and justice system. Muslim Turks, Arabs, and Iranians made up the early aristocracy that ruled during the fourteenth and fifteenth centuries. In addition, the Janissary Corps—drawn initially from Christian prisoners and slaves who were forced to convert to Islam and serve the sultan— were considered part of the ruling class.

The subject classes included Muslims as well as non-Muslim communities, which were known as *millets*. Non-Muslims were allowed to practice their own religion as long as they paid taxes to the Ottomans. Under this system, Jewish, Greek Orthodox, Armenian Gregorian, Roman Catholic, Protestant Christian, and Bulgarian Orthodox communities were allowed to follow some of their own religious laws, especially in matters relating to marriage, divorce, and inheritance.

As Suleyman's reign drew to an end, the empire grew increasingly chaotic. Overpopulation left a large part of the population with no work. Periods of famine and disease devastated wide areas. Bands of thieves attacked travelers as well as townspeople. The ruling classes grew more and more corrupt as they profited from the disorder in the empire.

While the Ottoman Empire was facing these internal challenges, the European kingdoms were growing stronger. Repeated efforts by the

Ottomans to gain control of Vienna were rebuffed. After a war with Austria from 1583 to 1599, the sultan was forced to recognize the Holy Roman Emperor as an equal. This marked a turning point in relations between Europe and the Ottoman Empire, because the Europeans realized how much the empire had declined. Using various treaties to their advantage, the Europeans were able to export goods to the Ottoman Empire and establish a trade advantage. Eventually, the increased European trade destroyed several craft industries in the empire, creating even more financial problems for the Ottomans.

Although efforts were made to reform the Ottoman power structure, none enjoyed long-term success. The eighteenth and nineteenth centuries were marked by continuous wars as European nations and

THE JANISSARY CORPS

As the Ottoman Empire expanded, a large army was required to maintain order. To fill this need, the government implemented a system called *devshirme,* which drafted Christians living in the empire to become soldiers and administrators. Those selected for the *devshirme* system were educated at the sultan's palace, and many later became military advisers.

Every three to five years, the sultan's scouts selected about 3,000 boys and young men to participate in the *devshirme* system. The boys had to be strong, healthy, and between the ages of eight and twenty. Orphans, only children, and married men were not subject to the *devshirme.*

The boys were taken to Istanbul and forced to convert to Islam. They were placed with Turkish families for several years to learn the Turkish language and customs. Once assimilated into the culture, the boys attended military schools in preparation for serving in the Janissary Corps or were placed in administrative positions in the palace and government.

The best and brightest were chosen to continue their education at the Enderun School. There they were educated in the

sciences, Turkish and Persian languages, literature, mathematics, and fine arts, including calligraphy, poetry, music, and drawing miniatures. Their physical training included archery, horseback riding, spear throwing, and wrestling. Finally, they were trained to serve the sultan. This training involved one to two years each in the Hawk Room, caring for the falcons and other birds used in hunting; the Wardrobe Room, caring for the sultan's clothing; the Butler's Room, supervising catering services; the Treasury Room, guarding the empire's valuables; and the Private Room, providing valet services for the sultan. Those who completed their service in the Private Room could be selected to serve in official state positions. By the time the Corps was disbanded in 1826, seventy-nine grand viziers and thirty-six navy admirals had been trained in the Janissary Corps.

Although the Janissary Corps enjoyed a high level of prestige, its members were, in truth, "slaves of the sultan's sword." Until the sixteenth century, Janissaries were not allowed to marry or own a business until they retired from the sultan's service.

Russia tried to take advantage of the Ottoman weakness. Rising nationalism encouraged Christian peoples in the European provinces of the Ottoman Empire (such as Greeks, Bulgarians, Romanians, and Serbs) to fight for their independence as well.

The Young Ottoman Movement

In the 1860s, a group called the Young Ottomans for a Constitution began demanding reforms in the Ottoman government. Made up primarily of intellectuals, the Young Ottomans wanted to limit the power of the ruling class by adopting a *constitution*—a written description of the country's laws and government processes. They also called for an elected parliament to represent the wishes of the people.

In 1876, Sultan Abdulhamid II accepted a constitution based on European models. It included provisions for an elected parliament, freedom of worship, and increased freedom of speech. Once securely in power as sultan, however, Abdulhamid suspended the constitution and ruled by decree. The Young Ottoman leaders were forced into exile, but continued to press for change through publications they sent to supporters in the empire.

The Young Turks

Abdulhamid's policies were denounced by many Ottoman subjects, even those in the military. Small groups of officers and students who opposed the sultan organized secret societies with the goal of restoring the constitution. These merged in 1907 to become the Committee of Union and Progress (CUP), commonly called the Young Turks. One of the leaders of the Young Turks was Mustafa Kemal.

In 1908, Ottoman armed forces demanded a return to constitutional government. Hoping to avoid being forced from office, Abdulhamid scheduled parliamentary elections later that year. Most seats in the parliament were won by CUP candidates, but differences of opinion about how to implement the government reform weakened their power. In 1909, Abdulhamid relinquished the throne to his brother, Mehmet V, who ruled for the next four years.

The instability in the Ottoman government during this period led to an upheaval in the provinces. European governments seized control of Ottoman lands in Europe, leaving only Thrace under Ottoman control. These losses propelled Enver Pasha to lead a coup against the liberal

Young Turks in power. The new government—led by Enver, Mehmet Talat Pasha, and Ahmet Cemal Pasha —soon ruled the empire as a military dictatorship.

World War I

As war between Germany and the Allied forces of Britain, France, and Russia became more likely in 1914, the Ottoman government considered remaining neutral. Past ties with Germany, however, led the Ottomans to align with Germany against the Allied powers. The Ottomans suffered staggering losses during the war, both within Anatolia and on the fronts. Nearly one-fourth of the population—about 6 million people—died during the war. Millions of these deaths were due to famine and disease.

An estimated 1 million Armenians died as a result of the forced evacuation of the Armenian population from eastern Anatolia, an event that has become known as the Armenian Massacre. Many Armenian men were killed as the soldiers forced them from their homes. The rest joined the women and children in a torturous wintertime march across

Although the Ottomans supported the Axis powers during World War I, the eventual defeat of the Axis paved the way for an independent Turkish nation.

thousands of miles without food, water, or shelter. Hundreds of thousands of the survivors of the march settled as refugees in other countries.

The Ottoman government denied charges of ethnic genocide, a claim that the Turkish government still echoes today. (*Genocide* is the systematic murder of people from a particular ethnic, racial, or religious group.) Rather, the Turkish government claims that the deportation of Armenians was ordered in response to an Armenian rebellion in which Armenians attacked and massacred Muslim villagers. The government blames the high number of deaths on the diseases and famine that were rampant during the war years.

The Birth of Modern Turkey

World War I ended in 1918 with the defeat of the Axis Powers. The Allies took control of the Ottoman Empire and planned to split it into new nations. The League of Nations, an international group that was a precursor to the United Nations, awarded mandates to European countries to govern the new nations established in the former Arab territories of the empire, until they were ready to govern themselves.

Before Allied plans for dividing Anatolia could be implemented, Mustafa Kemal (also known as Ataturk or "Father of the Turks")—one of

THE SIX ARROWS OF KEMALISM

Ataturk's reforms were based on a philosophy known as the "Six Arrows of Kemalism." They are written into Turkey's constitution.

- Republicanism—the belief that the people should have the ultimate power in government
- Nationalism—pride in the Turkish culture and belief that Turks should govern themselves without foreign intervention
- Populism—the belief that all citizens are equal and have the right to representation through the Grand National Assembly
- Reformism—the conviction that rapid transformation of society rested on the implementation of all reforms at once rather than piecemeal

- Statism—the involvement of the state in the economy to ensure rapid development
- Secularism—the separation of religion and state

Ataturk, created the modern state of Turkey with sweeping reforms that supported his vision of a national rather than religious identity for the country.

the outstanding Turkish military leaders during the war—pushed the League of Nations to recognize a Turkish republic. He argued that the predominantly Turkish-speaking areas of Anatolia and eastern Thrace should be part of an independent Turkish state. While the League considered this, Greece invaded western Anatolia, hoping to add that territory to its own.

Mustafa Kemal led Turkish troops in a War of Independence against Greece that lasted from 1919 to 1923. He also established a nationalist congress to create a National Pact, a document that relinquished claims to Arab provinces, guaranteed minority rights, and rejected any restrictions on the new nation. When the existing Ottoman parliament voted to accept the National Pact in 1920, the Allies moved in to seize public buildings and dismiss the parliament. The nationalists protested by convening a Grand National Assembly to elect Mustafa Kemal president. In 1921, the Grand National Assembly declared Turkey a sovereign nation.

After massacres in several Turkish villages by Greek forces in 1922, the Allies shifted their support from Greece to Turkey. Turkish nationalist forces finally succeeded in pushing the Greeks out of Anatolia. The Treaty of Lausanne, signed in 1923, established the right of Turkish areas in Anatolia and eastern Thrace to govern themselves. After the signing of the treaty, the Grand National Assembly abolished the sultanate and declared the Ottoman government extinct. Mustafa Kemal became the first president of the newly established Republic of Turkey.

The Reforms

The early years of the republic were marked by major reforms in every area of Turkish life. While the Ottomans had built their empire around Islam, Mustafa Kemal believed that the new nation must have a Turkish rather than an Islamic identity. He modeled the new republic after Western nations, believing that was the only path to becoming a modern nation.

The first major reform was to introduce a new legal code, modeled after those used in European countries. Under the new code, women were considered equal with men. Marriage and divorce were governed by civil code rather than religious law. Religious attire was outlawed in public, and people were encouraged to dress in the Western style. European naming conventions were adopted, which meant everyone had to adopt a surname. Language reforms were another monumental undertaking. Since the adoption of Islam by Turkish tribes in the tenth century, the Turkish language had been written in Arabic script. During the Ottoman period, many foreign words had been added to the Turkish language. Ataturk appointed a committee to adapt the Latin alphabet to the Turkish language and remove foreign words.

Although the legal and language reforms were far-reaching, the most drastic and controversial reforms were related to the *secularization* of the country, the removal of religion—in this case, Islam—from government, education, and the courts. Islam had been intertwined with government in Anatolia since the arrival of the Seljuks in the eleventh century. Now, despite protests from conservative Muslims, the caliphate was abolished, and religious schools were closed. Public readings of the Muslim holy book, the Qur'an (commonly known as the Koran in the West), and the call to worship were required to be in Turkish rather than the traditional Arabic. Women were not required to wear veils; in fact, they were not allowed to wear veils in government and other public buildings. Finally, the legal weekly holiday was changed from Friday—the Islamic holy day—to Sunday.

Adept at foreign relations, Ataturk kept his country at peace with its neighbors, providing the Turkish population with more settled times after decades of warfare and violence.

World War II

Ataturk died in 1938, on the eve of World War II (1939–1945). The new president, Ismet Inonu, and the Grand National Assembly were determined to keep Turkey out of the war if at all possible. When Germany invaded the Soviet Union, Turkey remained neutral. No Axis troops or supplies were allowed to cross Turkish territory, whether by ship, by plane, or overland. In 1945, as World War II drew to a close, Turkey declared war on Germany in order to participate in the Conference on International Organization that established the United Nations (UN). Because of its participation in that conference, Turkey became one of the fifty-one original members of the UN.

Political Change and Upheaval

Until the end of World War II, the Republican People's Party (Turkish acronym CHP) had been the only political party in Turkey. The end of the war brought a renewed interest in the private ownership of businesses, which was limited by the 1924 constitution. In 1946 a multiparty system was adopted, and the Democrat Party (DP) was founded with a goal of changing this provision of the constitution. The DP was quite successful in the 1950 election, winning a majority of seats in the assembly. Celal Bayar, one of the founders of the DP, was elected president and named Adnan Menderes prime minister. The new government introduced an economic policy designed to encourage private enterprise and foreign investment.

As the Cold War—the effort by the United States and its allies to stop the spread of Communism—heated up, Turkey aligned itself with the United States, receiving millions of dollars in financial aid under the Truman Doctrine and the Marshall Plan. Turkey joined the North Atlantic Treaty Organization (NATO) in 1952 and later became a member of the European Community, a trade organization that evolved into the European Union.

The DP gained even more parliamentary seats in 1954. The minority party, CHP, criticized the government's authoritarian and undemocratic attempts to limit the freedom of the press and restrict public assembly. Increasing violence against political leaders resulted in martial law being imposed in 1960. All political activity was suspended.

The Democrat Party (DP) first came to power in Turkey in 1950 under the leadership of Prime Minister Adnan Menderes (sixth from the left). Despite instituting many positive reforms, within ten years the charismatic leader seized control of the government, effectively forming a dictatorship. He and several cabinet members were tried and convicted of violating the constitution. Only Menderes was put to death.

Military leaders viewed the spreading rebellion with concern. Although Ataturk had been adamant that the military should not get involved in politics, most military leaders viewed the armed forces as the guardians of the constitution. Deciding that the Menderes government had abandoned Kemalist principles, the military seized government buildings. Military police arrested the president, prime minister, and other government officials, charging them with establishing a dictatorship. All were eventually tried and most were found guilty. Although fifteen were sentenced to death, only three, including former prime minister Menderes, were executed.

The Committee of National Unity (CNU), the military officers who had organized the coup, pledged to return the nation to civilian rule as soon as possible. In 1961 they drew up a new constitution that retained the Six Arrows of Kemalism but changed the structure of the parliament. The period after this constitution was ratified became known as the Second Republic. The CNU also established an economic development agency to address the high inflation rates and heavy debts that burdened the nation.

The Second Republic

Military control of the government ended with the 1961 elections. Fourteen political parties participated in this election, but candidates from only four parties won seats in the assembly. General Gursel, one of

Turkish citizens rejoice as General Cemal Gursel, leader of the coup that ousted Menderes, is elected president in 1961. Gursel was a great soldier and patriot who fought alongside Ataturk in Turkey's War of Independence (1920–1923).

the leaders of the 1960 coup, was elected president. The Justice Party—heir to many members of the now defunct DP—made a strong showing in the 1965 election, resulting in the naming of its leader, Suleyman Demirel, to the prime minister's position. Demirel enjoyed strong public support for the Justice Party's goal of open expression of Islam.

Conflict and tension simmered in Turkey in the 1960s and early 1970s. The Nationalist Action Party (Turkish acronym MHP) formed a paramilitary youth organization that escalated violence at political events. Protests against Turkey's alliances with the West gained strength. And the National Salvation Party (Turkish acronym MSP), which appeared on the political scene in 1970, advocated a return to Islamic principles in government.

The government became increasingly unstable following the 1969 elections, when major political parties lost seats in the assembly. Many Turks believed that the president and prime minister should step down, since their parties were no longer in control.

Increasing Violence

By 1971, the military grew concerned about the rising levels of violence in Turkey. Leaders sent the president a memorandum urging him to implement the reforms that were required in the 1961 constitution or else the military would take control of the government once again. Both the president and prime minister stepped down.

The parliament had difficulty electing a new president, casting fifteen ballots before selecting Fahri Koruturk. Koruturk was immediately faced with several problems that demanded resolution, most importantly the poor economy. Inflation and unemployment rates skyrocketed. The nation came very close to bankruptcy, saved only by loans from the International Monetary Fund. Amid the economic crisis were growing demands for an Islamic government. The fragmented parliament was unable to reach consensus on major issues. As a result, many political groups, including Kurdish nationalists, began using terrorism to achieve their goals.

The Cyprus problem resurfaced in 1974, when Greek Cypriots overthrew the government in an effort to force a political union with Greece. Koruturk's government, protesting the action, sent 40,000 troops to Cyprus to protect the Turkish Cypriots and expand the Turkish-occupied area. The UN negotiated a cease-fire, and in 1975, the Turkish

Federated State of Cyprus was founded in northern Cyprus (later the Turkish Republic of Northern Cyprus, or TRNC). To date, Turkey is the only nation to recognize the TRNC as an independent nation.

The 1980 Coup

Political volatility continued into the 1980s. When Koruturk retired as president in 1980, the parliament cast 100 ballots without choosing a replacement. Finally, the military stepped in and took control of the government again. Turkey was placed under martial law, all political activity was banned, and suspected terrorists were arrested. Members of the Grand National Assembly were banned from politics for up to ten years. Labor union strikes were banned, and freedom of the press was curtailed. As the crackdown continued, Western nations began to criticize the military government for human rights violations.

The leaders of the coup appointed a Consultative Assembly to create a new constitution. This constitution, approved by more than 90 percent of the voters in 1982, opened the door to the Third Republic of Turkey.

The Third Republic

Open elections were held in 1983, and a new civilian government was installed. The violence subsided, allowing the government to focus on economic reforms.

In 1990, the president of Iraq, Saddam Hussein, ordered his Iraqi troops to invade Kuwait. The UN immediately placed economic sanctions on Iraq, including a ban on exporting oil. Turkey, supporting the UN's actions, closed its pipeline to Iraq. Turkish troops joined an international coalition to force Iraq out of Kuwait, and Turkish military bases were opened to foreign troops.

The 1990s brought another round of economic ills. Tansu Ciller, the first female prime minister of Turkey, implemented an austerity program in an attempt to bring inflation under control. Among the steps taken to improve the economy was the privatization of several state-run industries.

In the mid-1990s, the Welfare Party, an Islamist group that called for an end to *secularism*, gained popularity. Its leader, Necmettin Erbakan, served as prime minister in 1996. He was forced to resign a year later by the military, and the Welfare Party was later banned by the Turkish courts.

Turkey Today

Ahmet Necdet Sezer, former chief justice of the constitutional court and a staunch defender of democracy, was elected president in 2000. Many view his election with both surprise and hope. Sezer is the first Turkish president who does not come from the military. Neither is he a career politician, another first. He supports secularism and has also spoken out against the 1980 constitution, saying that it does not support true democratic freedoms.

In 2002, the Islamist Justice and Development Party (Turkish acronym AK) gained the majority of seats in the parliament. The party's leader, Recep Tayyip Erdogan, was prohibited from taking political office because he had been convicted of inciting religious hatred after reading an Islamist poem at a political rally. Once the AK controlled the parliament, however, it changed the constitution to allow Erdogan to serve as prime minister.

As Turkish leaders work toward Turkey's acceptance into the European Union, they have loosened restrictions that once suppressed the Kurdish culture. In 2002, laws were passed that allow Kurdish parents to give their children Kurdish names. The Kurdish language may

Recep Tayyip Erdogan, prime minister of Turkey (left), and his deputy, Abdullah Gul, in 2002.

now be taught in schools. And a Kurdish broadcasting company has established a Kurdish television station.

When the United States prepared to invade Iraq and force Saddam Hussein from power in 2003, Turkey considered opening its bases to American troops. The parliament voted against that action, however. Several months into the war, Turkey offered to send troops to support U.S. military efforts in Iraq, but quickly withdrew the offer when the Iraqi Governing Council voiced concerns about having Turkish troops in Iraq.

Economy

Turkey's economy is among the most diversified in the Middle East. Modern industries such as textile and clothing manufacturing are growing rapidly. At the same time, traditional agriculture employs about 40 percent of the Turkish workforce. Many industries remain under state control, although new government regulations encourage the development of the private sector.

Interspersed with periods of intense economic growth have been severe economic crises. In 1980, the government was unable to make payments on its huge debts and the economy collapsed. Changes in economic policy

Turkey has a broad base of industry. The iron and steel industries generate a great deal of income for the country.

helped businesses begin to grow once again, but in 1994, inflation soared to 150 percent. (When inflation is present, goods cost more to purchase.) The crisis was eventually resolved and inflation was brought under control, but many workers lost their jobs or had their salaries reduced.

Despite the rapid growth of some industries, high unemployment remains a problem due to the soaring birthrate in recent decades. Many Turks have emigrated to other countries in search of work, with most settling in Germany, Belgium, Switzerland, and Sweden. The money they send home helps support their families, who often remain in Turkey.

Business and Industry

Economic crises in the 1980s and again in 1994 punctured Turkey's periods of rapid business expansion. After the collapse of the Soviet Union in 1991, Turkey seized the opportunity to become a regional leader by organizing the Black Sea Economic Cooperation Summit. This meeting between the leaders of Turkey, Greece, and nine former Soviet countries established a regional economic organization that promotes free trade among member nations. This agreement, along with Turkey's "custom integration" with the European Union that was granted in 1996, has opened many new markets for Turkish goods.

Agriculture

With thousands of acres of fertile soil and an accommodating climate, Turkey produces enough food to be self-sufficient. Major crops include grains such as wheat, barley, and rice; fruits such as cherries, apricots, kiwi, and olives; and cotton and tobacco. Tea and hazelnuts are grown in the Black Sea region, which receives more rain than any other part of Turkey. Cotton, tobacco, dried fruits, and nuts are exported to countries in the European Union and the United States, while many Middle Eastern countries import a wide variety of fresh vegetables, fruits, and meats from Turkey.

Although over half of Turkey's workforce is in agriculture, it generates less income than other sectors. Many farmers continue to use traditional methods of farming on small plots, even though modern techniques could improve production. The labor-intensive nature of farming and the low-income levels have pushed many young people out of the rural areas and into the cities. Many end up living in slums, unable to find work in the factories.

Manufacturing

One of the most important goals of the founders of the Republic of Turkey was to create a thriving industrial base that could help modernize the country. In the 1930s, Ataturk's government established state-run factories in an effort to promote more rapid industrial development. Turkey experienced a period of rapid industrial growth between 1950 and 1977. However, energy shortages combined with other factors to cause a sharp decline in productivity in the 1980s. Many of the country's first industries were operated by the state, but by the early 1990s, the government had moved to privatize state-owned industries.

Today, Turkey has a broad base of industries. The food-processing, petroleum, textiles, and iron and steel industries generate the most income; other important industries produce chemicals, cement, fertilizer, automobiles, electronics, and software. Many of these industries rely upon minerals mined in Turkey, such as chromium, bauxite, copper, and iron.

Tourism

Turkey has much to offer tourists: coastal areas with pristine waters and luxurious resorts, stunning mountains and lakes, thousands of historical sites, and relatively low prices. It wasn't until the 1980s, when the government began marketing Turkey's attractions, that large numbers of tourists started choosing Turkey as a holiday destination. Today, most people visiting Turkey come from Europe, the former Soviet republics, and the Middle East.

Building the tourist industry hasn't been easy, however. Ongoing conflicts between the Kurds and the government have had an adverse effect on tourism, as has the volatile political situation in the Middle East. Natural disasters such as earthquakes have also affected tourism. After a deadly earthquake in 1999 near Istanbul, tourism levels fell for some time. Even more chilling was the explosion of the Chernobyl nuclear reactor in nearby Ukraine in 1986. Radioactive fallout from the accident drifted into western Turkey, contaminating crops and thus the food supply.

Media and Communications

Turkey has a very active media market. The government broadcasts news and cultural and educational programming on both radio and television. In addition, there are about 300 privately owned television stations and over a thousand independent radio broadcasters. There are also numerous newspapers and magazines.

The government heavily censors Turkish media. Articles or news reports critical of government policies or the military may result in arrest and a jail term. The Kurdish situation and the rise of Islam in politics are also sensitive subjects. Television networks that air controversial programming can be shut down by the government. Until 2002, Turkish broadcasters could not air any programming in Kurdish. Despite the ban, many Kurds were able to watch Kurdish programming via satellite.

Religion and Beliefs

When the republic was established in 1923, Kemal Ataturk instituted far-ranging reforms in his effort to modernize Turkey. The most controversial was the complete separation of religion and government—

Although Turkey is a secular state, religious convictions and traditions remain strong among its population.

the secularization of Turkey. No longer would the political leader of
Turkey claim to be the religious leader of all Muslims. Islamic law was
replaced with *secular* laws based on Western models. Religious clothing
was prohibited except in places of worship. The Turkish language
replaced Arabic as the language of religion. The education system was
removed from the control of Islamic leaders and placed under the
supervision of the state, which prohibited religious education for a
period. Turkey is the only Middle Eastern country to implement such a
radical program of secularization.

While most of the educated elite favored these changes, they were
not always well accepted by the general population, especially in the
rural areas. By the 1980s, there was a deep division in Turkish society
regarding the place of religion in government. A growing number of
political leaders have challenged secular policies in recent years, thus
generating an Islamic revival in Turkey.

Religious freedom is guaranteed in the Turkish constitution.
Although nearly all Turks are Muslims, there are many different Islamic
sects in Turkey. About 80 percent of all Muslims follow Sunni (SOO-
nee) traditions, the largest branch of Islam worldwide. Within this
group, however, beliefs range from conservative to liberal. About one-
fifth of all Sunnis in Turkey practice Sufism (SOO-fih-zum), a mystical
approach to Islam. An estimated 20 percent of Turkish Muslims belong
to Shi'ite (SHEE-ite) Muslim sects or to sects whose faith combines
Islamic beliefs with those of other religions. Less than 1 percent of the
population follows a religion other than Islam.

Islam

All Muslims follow the teachings of the Prophet Mohammad, who
established Islam in the seventh century. They believe in one God—
Allah—who revealed the Qur'an to Mohammad, the last in a series of
prophets that includes Abraham and Jesus. Devout Muslims fulfill the
religious duties, known as the five pillars of Islam, outlined in the
Qur'an: professing that "there is no God but God and Mohammad is his
messenger," praying five times daily, fasting during the holy month of
Ramazan (called Ramadan by most Muslims), giving alms (charity) to
the poor, and making a pilgrimage to Mecca, the birthplace of
Mohammad. (To learn more about Islam, see pages ix–xii in the
introduction to this volume.)

Branches of Islam

After Mohammad's death, the Islamic community was divided about how to select a *caliph,* or successor. Most wanted the whole community to select a caliph. Some believed that Ali, Mohammad's son-in-law and cousin, should assume the leadership of the Islamic community. Over the next century, this disagreement about how to select successors deepened. Eventually, the traditionalists became known as Sunni Muslims, while those who believed that Ali and his descendants were the rightful Islamic leaders were called Shi'a Muslims or Shi'ites. Most Muslims around the world and in Turkey follow the Sunni branch of Islam.

SUFISM

Sufism is a mystical movement within Islam. It began in the earliest days of Islam, when companions of Mohammad met at the platform in Medina where he prayed to discuss the meaning of Qur'anic verses and disciplines that would lead to inner knowledge. They became known as the Ahle-Suffa, the people of the platform.

Sufis (SOO-fees) dedicate themselves to meditation, purification, and service in order to seek a better understanding of the reality of God and the relationship between God and humans. Because Sufis believe that people cannot achieve oneness with God through language and logic alone, music and dance are often included as part of the meditative service. This is in direct conflict with strict orthodox Muslim beliefs that music should have no role in religious services.

One of the best-known Sufi brotherhoods—the Mevlevi, or whirling dervishes—was established in Anatolia in the thirteenth century. Today, the Mevlevi brotherhood is based in Konya, Turkey. Mevlevis dress in white robes with white jackets and white cone-shaped hats. With their right hands reaching toward heaven and their left hands pointing toward earth, the Mevlevis spin and whirl to music played on traditional instruments, including the

ney—a bamboo flute—and the *kudum*—a small kettledrum. Their robes flare out as they revolve around the room, chanting and singing to increase their awareness of God.

The religious reforms enacted by Ataturk made sects such as the Mevlevi illegal. Although the dervishes continued their traditions, they no longer did so openly. Today, the Mevlevi are allowed to perform in public during the Mevlana Festival, which honors the founder of the brotherhood, Persian poet Jelaleddin Rumi, also known as the Mevlana. Sufis from many different countries attend the festival, which is held in Konya each year.

Whirling dervishes from Konya perform their Mevlevi Order Sufi Ritual in exhibitions throughout the world, but can perform their traditional dance in public in Turkey only at the annual festival of Mevlana.

Within the Shi'ite community, further differences developed. Most Shi'ites believed that there were twelve *imams*—religious leaders descended from Mohammad and Ali who had divine authority to interpret the Qur'an. These Shi'ites were known as the Jafari, or Twelver, Shi'ites. Others in the Shi'ite community—the Ismailis—traced the descendants of Ali differently, recognizing seven *imams*. About one-fifth of the Shi'ite Muslims in Turkey are believed to belong to the Twelver sect.

In Turkey, most Shi'ite Muslims belong to the Alevi sect, an offshoot of the Twelver Shi'ites. (In Syria, the Alevi are known as the Alawites.) The Alevis believe that Mohammad's son-in-law Ali was a prophet like Mohammad and, as such, was the rightful successor to Mohammad. While they recognize the five pillars of Islam, Alevis believe that these are symbolic rather than required duties. They also add two additional pillars: *jihad,* or struggle, and *waliya,* loyalty to Ali.

In addition to observing Islamic holidays such as Sheker Bayrami and Kurban Bayrami, the Alevis celebrate the Christian holy days of Christmas and Epiphany. They also observe No-Ruz, an ancient celebration of spring and the new year that originated with the Zoroastrians of Iran. Because of their observance of other religious traditions and refusal to treat the five pillars of Islam as religious duties, the Alevis have faced high levels of persecution from conservative Sunni Muslims throughout history. In Turkey, many Alevis were killed during religious riots in the 1970s and early 1990s.

Most Alevis are originally from southeastern Turkey, but many Alevi communities are scattered throughout the country today. Although no census figures related to religion or ethnicity have been available since 1965, scholars believe that ethnic Turks make up the majority of the Alevi sect.

UNORTHODOX BELIEFS

Turkey is home to a small number of Yazidis, members of an unorthodox Islamic sect. Sometimes called devil worshipers by orthodox Muslims, the Yazidis combine beliefs from Zoroastrianism (an ancient Persian religion), Christianity, Islam, and ancient pagan religions.

Members of another unorthodox group, called the Donme, follow both Jewish and Islamic traditions. They consider themselves Muslims, but they have not been accepted historically by either the Muslims or the Jews.

Other Religions

During the Byzantine era, present-day Turkey was predominantly Christian, and Constantinople (present-day Istanbul) was the center of the Eastern Orthodox Church. Even under Ottoman rule, large numbers of Christians lived in Anatolia. Today, however, less than 100,000 Christians make their home in Turkey. Most of these Christians live in Istanbul or Ankara and belong to the Roman Catholic Church, the Greek Orthodox Church, or the Russian Orthodox Church. The patriarch (leader) of the Greek Orthodox Church still maintains his headquarters in Istanbul.

Although there were large communities of Jews living in Anatolia during the Ottoman period, many immigrated to Israel when it became an independent nation in 1948. Today, fewer than 20,000 Jews live in Turkey, most in Istanbul or Ankara.

Everyday Life

Day-to-day life in Turkey can vary quite dramatically depending upon where one lives. Members of the upper and middle classes in urban areas are similar in many respects to their counterparts in Western cities. Those living in rural areas have maintained a much more traditional culture, especially regarding roles for men and women.

Family Life

Kemal Ataturk's secular reforms transformed Turkish society, affecting the family structure that was prevalent in Turkey at the time. Under Islam, men could take up to four wives and later divorce them simply by renunciation. Women could testify in court, but their testimony was given only half the weight of a man's testimony. The implementation of a secular legal code in the 1920s changed all this. Polygamy was outlawed, and marriage and divorce became a civil rather than religious matter. Women were given equal rights, including equal access to education.

Women in urban areas could easily take advantage of these new opportunities. Literacy rates for women rose, and their political involvement increased. Today, about one-third of Turkey's medical doctors and university professors are women, as are about one-fourth of the country's lawyers and judges. At the same time, women in rural areas continue to be constrained by tradition, the economy, and other factors. About one-third of the women in eastern and southeastern

Turkey are illiterate. They often work on the family farm. With little education or industry in the region, there are few opportunities for them outside the home.

Although equal rights for women have been a goal since the republic was founded in 1923, Turkey still has a male-dominated society. The man remains the head of the family, making all the important decisions for the family group. Although many women work outside the home to help support the family, the men—especially in rural areas or in the urban lower class—still typically determine how the money will be spent.

In rural regions, extended families composed of grandparents, parents, and children often share a house. They work together on the family farm or in jobs in the village. While the father is expected to support the family financially, others in the household contribute income when they are able. Women typically take care of the home and children. In the past, a woman had to ask her husband's permission to work outside the home, but the parliament has discussed a law that would eliminate this requirement.

Although extended families have traditionally been the norm in Turkey, nuclear families are becoming increasingly common due to the migration from rural to urban areas. Several factors influence this trend, including the ongoing housing shortage.

WOMEN IN POLITICS

Turkish women proudly point out that they have had the right to vote since 1923, longer than women in some European countries. However, female political representatives in parliament continue to be quite rare. Some women attribute this to the political parties themselves, arguing that women who want to run for office are offered as candidates in precincts that the party does not expect to carry. Women's groups are beginning to form coalitions to pressure the political parties to improve their record regarding women. The coalitions have implemented grassroots campaigns to convince women to vote for a political party based on the number of female candidates it allows to run for office as well as on its policies regarding women's issues.

The increasing presence of women and their desire for representation in politics and government in Turkey can be felt throughout the country.

Dress

Traditional Anatolian clothing varies from region to region, but the costumes share some similarities. Women generally wear baggy pants called *salvar,* a shirt called a *mintan,* and up to three brightly colored skirts. Embroidered designs are often unique to a particular village or region. Traditional headdresses for women are heavily ornamented. The way in which they are worn and their design indicates a woman's social position: whether she is married, engaged, single, or widowed, and whether she has children.

Today, these traditional costumes are rarely seen outside of folk festivals or folk-dancing exhibitions. Women in rural areas may still wear some types of traditional clothing, but most women in urban areas wear Western-style clothing.

The veil worn by women in many Muslim countries is not required in Turkey. In fact, women are prohibited from wearing a veil in public buildings such as a government office or university, a result of the secular reforms. Today, however, the veil is gaining favor in Turkish society. Some groups are working to change the laws so that women who wish to wear veils may do so in public buildings.

Traditional clothing for men has just about disappeared in all parts of Turkey, replaced by typical Western-style attire. The traditional costume, which varied by region, typically included baggy pants known as *salvar,* a collarless shirt, and a *cepken,* a vest or short jacket with slit sleeves.

Before the founding of the republic, men often wore a type of brimless velvet hat called a *fez.* These were outlawed in 1925, and men were encouraged to wear a fedora or other type of hat instead.

Education

Under the republic, a free education is guaranteed to every citizen. There has been difficulty in achieving this goal, however, especially in the rural areas. While classes from kindergarten to high school are available in urban areas, many rural villages have only elementary schools. Many families cannot afford the cost of their children's commuting to another town or sending their children to live in a city in order to finish their education. In addition, children living in rural areas are often needed to work on their family's farm. In some regions, school schedules now accommodate the planting and harvesting seasons.

The educational system is divided into elementary schools serving children ages six to eleven, middle schools for youth from twelve to fourteen, and high schools and *lycées* (lee-SAYS) for older teens. School is required for students between six and fourteen. Those students who continue their education may choose to attend a high school, which teaches vocational or general education classes, or a lycée, which provides a college preparatory course. All education below the university level is free.

When the secular reforms were implemented in the 1920s, the schools were removed from the supervision of Islamic authorities. Religious education in school was banned at this time, but later it was allowed in the primary grades. There are increasing calls to restore religious education in the schools at all levels. In the meantime, many towns and villages offer informal religious classes.

Turkey has over twenty universities and many other higher education facilities for those students who want to continue their education. Several new private universities that were established in the last decade have attracted growing numbers of teachers and students.

Recreation and Leisure

The Turkish people enjoy a wide range of sports and activities during their leisure time. Some sports, like soccer and badminton, are quite common in the West. Other activities, such as greased wrestling, are unique to Turkey.

Sports

Of the many sports that are popular in Turkey, soccer is perhaps the favorite. Each village and town that is able to pull a team together does so. There is also a national team that competes in international events. Soccer fans take the games very seriously, and incidents of violence during and after games are becoming more common. Gambling is also developing into a problem. Large amounts of money are often involved, and sometimes bribes are offered to players and managers to deliberately lose a game.

In addition to soccer, many other modern sports are common in Turkey. Among them are volleyball, basketball, mountaineering, fencing, rowing, table tennis, karate, swimming, car racing, and archery. The Turkish military sponsors some sports clubs, as do other organizations.

One sport that is unique to Turkey is greased wrestling. Each year, the three-day Kirkpinar Wrestling Tournament is held in Edirne, near the border of Bulgaria. Over a thousand wrestlers enter the tournament each year, hoping to win the grand prize of a gold belt. In this sport, which dates back over six centuries, wrestlers wear leather breeches and oil their bodies with olive oil before beginning a match. The best wrestlers may fight for several hours before a winner is declared.

Cirit (jer-IT) is another sport that dates back to the Ottoman period. Originally a military exercise to improve equestrian skills, *cirit* became a popular spectator sport. Two teams of horsemen line up opposite each other on a field. Each man carries a wooden stick about 3 feet (1 meter) long and an inch (2.5 centimeters) in diameter. To start a round, a player rides toward the opposing team and throws his stick at one of the players. He then must ride back to his team while trying to avoid getting hit by the other player, who still has his stick. The best *cirit* players are able to elude their pursuers by dropping to the side of their horse and using other acrobatic riding techniques. At the end of the game, the team that has scored the most hits wins. Although this sport is not as widespread as it once was, many folklore societies are keeping it alive through organized tournaments.

Ataturk (Father of the Turks) said that "intelligent minds house themselves in healthy bodies." Turks are proud of their country's emphasis on sport, from the national game of football (soccer) to the time-honored ancient sport of greased wrestling.

Socializing

Aside from sports, many Turks enjoy socializing with friends and family members during their time away from work. Most social activities in Turkish villages are traditionally segregated by gender. The men often gather at community buildings or teahouses to play backgammon or discuss politics, while the women, who rarely go out in public, socialize with family and female friends in their homes.

Food

Turkish cuisine reflects the wide variety of foods that are available in the country. With many different climates and an abundance of fertile soil and water, Turkey is able to grow many different types of foods. The hillsides and valleys in the west produce many types of fruits and vegetables. The Eastern Highlands are better suited to raising livestock, so meat and milk products are more common there. The coastal regions depend upon a variety of fish and seafood. In addition, the Black Sea region grows hazelnuts and corn. A small anchovy-like fish called *hamsi* is used in many dishes. Each region has developed its own specialties, based on what is grown in the area.

The spiciest foods come from southeastern Turkey, which has a desert climate. The spices may have originally been added to slow down spoilage in the hot weather.

The culinary center of the country is the Marmara region, which includes Istanbul. The land is very fertile, and many different types of fruits and vegetables are grown there. Many chefs believe that lamb from this area has a more delicate flavor than any other.

Most Turkish families eat all their meals together. If other family members are not home, most Turks will wait to eat rather than eating alone. The Turkish word for breakfast, *kahvalti,* means literally "foundation for coffee." It is usually a small meal of bread, cheese, and olives. Lunch is also light, consisting of dishes such as stuffed cabbage leaves or a type of pizza called *pide.*

Dinner is the main meal of the day, served late in the evening. The meal starts with *meze* (MAY-zay), an array of appetizers. Feta cheese and melon slices are almost always served as meze. Green salads,

Did You Know?

Although Islam forbids the consumption of both alcohol and pork, wine and beer are commonly served in Turkey. The national drink, *raki,* is an alcoholic beverage. While many Muslims consume alcohol, most follow the prohibition against pork.

vegetables sautéed in olive oil, fried mussels or calamari, and fish eggs are often served before meals featuring fish or grilled meats. If kebab is planned for the main dish, then the meze will include small dishes of hummus (a dip made from chickpeas), beans, eggplant, mushrooms, tomatoes, pickles, and stuffed grape leaves. Raki—the anise-flavored national drink of Turkey—is usually served with meze.

Following the meze, the main meal is served. It usually includes bread or another food made from grains, vegetables, and a meat dish. Bread is usually purchased at the neighborhood bakery each day. Other foods in the bread category include *manti,* dumplings filled with meat and served in a garlic sauce, and *borek,* thin sheets of dough that are folded into shapes and filled with cheeses or meats. *Pilaf* made from cracked wheat or rice and cooked with an assortment of vegetables is often served as a complete meal.

Turkish cuisine features many vegetables. One common way of preparing vegetables is to simmer them with tomatoes, onions, and peppers. Pumpkins, squash, eggplant, peppers, or tomatoes are stuffed

Did You Know?

During the Ottoman period, one of the tests of a cook's skill was preparing baklava. The best cooks could layer 100 sheets of ultrathin pastry in a tray, separated by syrup and nuts. When the baklava was finished baking, a gold coin was dropped from 18 inches (46 centimeters) above the tray. If the coin did not slice through the pastry sheets and hit the tray, the cook was disgraced.

CACIK (CHILLED YOGURT AND CUCUMBER SOUP)

Cacik is similar to the yogurt and cucumber salads prepared in Lebanon, Syria, Cyprus, and Greece, except it is thinned down and eaten as a soup.

2 small green cucumbers, peeled
1 teaspoon salt
3 cups plain yogurt
2 cloves garlic, crushed
2 tablespoons fresh mint, finely chopped
1 tablespoon fresh dill, finely chopped (optional)
3 tablespoons olive oil
1 cup iced water
Freshly ground white pepper
Salt
Thin cucumber slices, to garnish
Mint springs, to garnish

Shred cucumber into colander and lightly mix in salt. Let stand 20 minutes to drain. Transfer the cucumber to a large bowl and add the yogurt, garlic, mint, dill, and olive oil. Cover and refrigerate at least 2 hours.

Just before serving, add iced water until soup is creamy, but not too thin. Depending upon the thickness of yogurt, you may not need to use all the water. Add pepper and salt to taste. Garnish with cucumber slices and mint.

Source: Adapted from *The Complete Mediterranean Cookbook* by Tess Mallos.

with meat and rice fillings to create a main dish. These stuffed vegetables are known as *dolmas.*

Meat, fish, or poultry is an important part of the meal, but not the centerpiece. Meat is used sparingly, to provide flavor to dishes. One exception is the meat dish commonly associated with Turkey: *kebab* (keh-BAHB), or meat roasted on a skewer. There are two main categories of kebab, shish kebab and doner kebab. *Shish kebab* is prepared by grilling small cubes of meat on a skewer; for *doner kebab*, alternating layers of ground beef and lamb are arranged on a large upright skewer and roasted by rotating the skewer in front of a vertical grill. As the meat browns, thin slices are shaved off and served with melted butter and pita bread.

> *Choose your friends by the taste of their food.*
>
> —Turkish proverb

Fresh seasonal fruit is typically served at the end of a meal. The sweets most often associated with Turkey—Turkish delight and baklava—are not usually eaten at the end of a meal. Rather, they are generally enjoyed as a snack with coffee.

Holidays and Festivals

Despite being a secular state, Turkey's most important holidays—Sheker Bayrami and Kurban Bayrami—are religious celebrations. Many national holidays and cultural festivals are celebrated as well.

Islamic Celebrations

The festivities of Sheker Bayrami—the Sugar Festival—begin at the end of Ramazan (Ramazan is the Turkish name for Ramadan), Islam's holiest month. (Sheker Bayrami is known as Eid al-Fitr in Arabic.) After fasting from sunrise until sunset every day during Ramazan, Muslims eagerly anticipate the feasts and activities of Sheker Bayrami (SHEH-ker bah-hee-rah-muh). Families and close friends gather for lavish feasts, where special sweets associated with Ramazan, such as baklava, are served. Children receive gifts of money and candy. Traditional Turkish music and folk dancing are often a part of the three-day national holiday, as are greased wrestling matches.

Kurban Bayrami (koor-BAHN bah-hee-rah-muh) takes place during the *hajj* or pilgrimage season. This Feast of the Sacrifice (Eid al-Adha in Arabic) honors Abraham's obedience to God. Because Abraham was willing to sacrifice his son to God, God allowed Abraham to sacrifice a lamb instead. Traditionally, each family slaughters a sheep at the beginning of Kurban Bayrami and shares the meat with relatives and with the poor. In Turkey, this national holiday lasts four to five days.

Because Sheker Bayrami and Kurban Bayrami are observed according to the Islamic calendar, the actual dates for the holidays change every year.

Festivals and National Holidays

The Kurdish New Year—Newroz—is March 21, the spring equinox. Until recently, celebrations of this holiday were illegal. In 1995, however, Prime Minister Tansu Ciller declared that Newroz had roots in ancient Turkish culture, thus clearing the way for traditional celebrations to be held. Traditionally, special foods are prepared for the holiday, and there is much visiting between family and friends. Events held in conjunction with Newroz are subject to heavy security by the Turkish military, and clashes between the Kurds and military are common.

The International Istanbul Festival draws thousands of performers and visitors each summer. The venues are as exciting as the programs, with performances held at historical sites such as the Topkapi Palace.

Legalized celebration of Newroz is just one of the reforms the Kurdish people have fought for over the years.

Presentations of ballet, opera, and classical music alternate with Turkish folk music and dances.

Another popular cultural attraction is the Mevlana Festival, which is held in Konya each December. Sufi followers from around the world attend the festival. It is the one time of the year that the whirling dervishes are allowed to perform in public.

Many of Turkey's national holidays commemorate events associated with the founding of the republic. National Independence and Children's Day celebrates the first meeting of the Grand National Assembly; Victory Day marks Turkey's victory against Greece in the War of Independence (1919–1922); and Republic Day commemorates the proclamation that established the nation. Most Turks also observe the anniversary of Kemal Ataturk's death, even though it isn't a national holiday.

The Arts

Throughout its recorded history, the artisans living in the region that is now called Turkey have been renowned for their beautiful craftwork and

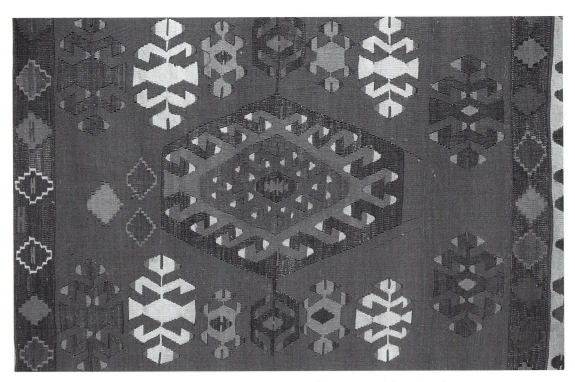

Kilim rugs from Turkey are found in many European and American homes.

paintings. Performers—from storytellers and puppet masters to dancers and musicians—have played an important role in Turkish culture as well. Today's art scene is as vibrant as ever, with both traditional and contemporary offerings. Western-style music, dance, and theater are all readily available.

Traditional Crafts

Many of the traditional art forms in Turkey today have been practiced for centuries. A thriving handcraft industry produces carpets, pottery, leather, and the brass and copper objects found in most bazaars. These skills, along with decorative arts techniques such as enameling and repoussé, have been handed down from generation to generation.

Carpets

Turkish carpet makers' skills have been admired for thousands of years. In fact, archaeological excavations in central Anatolia have found carbonized rug fragments dating back 9,000 years. Today's carpet makers still use many of the same patterns that were created in ancient times.

Some Turkish carpets are knotted, similar in construction to those made in Iran. In the best carpets, each square inch holds thousands of knots, creating intricate patterns and a plush pile. Most carpets are made of wool, but sometimes cotton or silk is used. The finished carpets are used as home furnishings or for religious purposes, to decorate mosques or as prayer rugs for individuals.

Another type of Turkish carpet is known as *kilim* (KEE-lim)—flat, carpets woven on looms rather than knotted. These are usually functional pieces, often used as blankets, curtains, or slipcovers for furniture. Kilims are generally quite colorful, with highly stylized geometric patterns, and embroidery is sometimes added.

All Turkish weavers are women. They create their own designs, which are often influenced by traditional designs unique to their region. Some patterns are found throughout Turkey and have changed very little since Ottoman times. Interestingly, although men do not weave carpets, most carpet repairs and retail sales are made by men.

Ceramic Arts

Fine ceramics have been produced in Anatolia, especially in the cities of Iznik and Kutahya, since ancient times. Best known are the enameled tiles that were used to decorate mosques, dervish lodges, Turkish baths, kiosks, palaces, fountains, and churches. However, plates, bowls, vases, and other functional pieces were also created.

Colors and patterns are often used to date the tiles in historical buildings. The earliest designs were blue and white, but by the mid-sixteenth century other colors had been added. The classical *rumi* designs use palm and lotus motifs in green, yellow, and dark blue.

Blue *Iznik* tile comes from west central Anatolia. The materials and methods used to create this tile were developed in the city of Iznik over 400 years ago. This tile is used primarily to decorate mosques and public buildings. The Blue Mosque in Istanbul is famous for its use of blue Iznik tiles.

Today, much of the pottery made in Turkey comes from the city of Kutahya. It is famous for its blue and green pieces that are still created following an ancient process. They are decorated with birds, flowers, or pastel designs. In the markets today are pieces with creative designs that fuse new patterns and colors with traditional styles.

The artisans creating Iznik tile today use the same creative and production processes developed 400 years ago.

Metalwork

Turkish artisans have long been known for their work in metal. The earliest artisans worked with copper and brass, and later with silver and gold. Although decorative pieces are still made with these metals, handmade pieces are increasingly rare.

In the past, many Turkish artists produced exquisitely decorated metal items using a technique called *repoussé*. This technique allows artists to create raised designs by working thin sheets of gold, silver, or copper from the back. The background is then lowered around the design using engraving tools and a hammer. Traditionally, items such as jewelry, candlesticks, pitchers, drums, and even fountains were adorned with plant, animal, and geometric motifs using *repoussé*.

Today, *repoussé* is almost a lost art. Commercially produced metal items that, at first glance, look similar to those made with *repoussé* have nearly priced true *repoussé* pieces out of the market. However, these look-alikes are mass-produced using molds and stamps, not traditional *repoussé*. Two contemporary artists among the few who are keeping this art alive are Ziaya Oygan and Huseyin Azmi Baykal. Many fear that *repoussé* will vanish if steps are not taken to make sure it is taught correctly.

> ### *Did You Know?*
> Turkey is the only country in the world that has large enough deposits of *meerschaum*—a white, absorbent clay—to exploit it commercially. The clay is made into pipes, cigarette holders, and other decorative items.

Visual Arts

Turkey has a rich tradition of visual arts as well. Miniatures are one of the oldest surviving visual arts in Turkey. Wall paintings dating back to the eighth and ninth centuries illustrate scenes from nomadic life as well as fantastical worlds. Turkish miniature painters were sponsored by the Ottoman sultans, and a distinct style developed. European visitors to Anatolia often hired local bazaar artists to accompany them on their travels through the region. The sketches and miniatures of their journeys provide an interesting glimpse back in time.

The art of *ebru* (marbled paper) also developed during the Ottoman era. *Ebru* is a technique used to create colorful patterns on paper. Artists start with a shallow pan of oily water, then add paints to the surface. Designs are created in the paints using special brushes; then paper is gently laid on the painted surface of the tray and carefully lifted off. It is believed that the *ebru* process was invented in the thirteenth century. During the Seljuk and Ottoman period, *ebru* was used to decorate the sultans' books, decrees, correspondence, and other documents.

Painting in the European style gained popularity during the mid-1800s and has continued to evolve over the years. Since many of the early artists studied in Europe, they were influenced by Western trends, such as impressionism, and later cubism and expressionism. By the 1950s, some artists were adding Turkish folkloric elements to their work, fusing international trends with Turkish tradition.

Performing Arts

As in other areas of the arts, Turkey's rich past in the performing arts informs its contemporary offerings. Music, dance, theatrical performances, and film are all part of modern Turkish culture, and most have deep roots in the past.

Music

Many forms of music are performed in Turkey today, from classical Turkish to folk music to Western-style pop and classical. What is generally known as Turkish classical music today evolved from the Ottoman classical music that developed centuries ago. It includes both songs and elaborate instrumental pieces played by ensembles of traditional instruments (lutes, fiddles, zithers, flutes, and drums). Most classical music is composed around three central themes: love, war, and religion. The music incorporates influences from Arab, Persian, and Balkan traditions encountered in the provinces of the vast empire.

The folk music of Anatolia is very rich, with repertoires and performance styles varying between regions. It is usually sung by *asiks,* or folk poets, as they pluck the strings of the *saz,* a long-necked lute with three sets of metal strings. The neck of the *saz* is about twice as long as the body of the instrument. This traditional instrument is still very popular in Turkey, with new styles of construction and innovative performance techniques being developed for it. The *asiks* sing songs about life and love, betrayal, and hopes for a rich harvest.

Mevlevi music is another category of Turkish music. It describes the music that accompanies the meditative dance of the Mevlevi brotherhood, or the whirling dervishes. The music is classical; in fact, many of the leading composers and performers of Ottoman classical music were members of the Mevlevi order. Two instruments in particular are used in Mevlevi music: the *ney*, a bamboo flute with six finger holes in front and one thumbhole in back, and the *kudum*, a type of kettledrum, usually played in pairs.

Dance

Many folk songs have traditional folk dances that accompany them. These folk dances have their roots in the ancient past, long before the Turks converted to Islam. Some feature both male and female dancers, while other dances are performed by men only. The dances vary by region and even by village. Dancers wearing costumes unique to their region often perform at weddings, festivals, and other joyful occasions.

Classical ballet was introduced in Turkey in 1948, when the first school was established. Over the past five and a half decades, ballet has gained wider acceptance. Today, several Turkish ballets have been written and performed. Many of them feature elements of Turkish folk dances and music.

Theater and Film

Traditional Turkish theater offerings include *Karagoz* (shadow plays), puppet shows, and *meddahlik*. The shadow plays are named for one of the main characters, Karagoz, who teaches an amusing lesson in each performance. Each show is performed by one artist who moves the shadow figures and voices the various characters' roles.

The traditional art of shadow puppet theater is very popular during Ramazan, when Turkish Muslims, who have fasted all day, celebrate and rejoice after their evening meal.

Puppet shows are another form of traditional theater, having been performed since the 1300s. Various types of puppets are used in the shows, including marionette-style puppets, hand puppets, and chair puppets. The puppet shows focus on topics of everyday life or retell literary stories. Although few artists perform traditional puppet shows today, a small number of individuals have revived the art.

Meddahlik refers to the art of the storyteller, or *meddah*. These one-person shows regale audiences with retellings of folk tales, legends, and episodes from daily life. The stories are typically very funny and end with a moral. The traditional *meddahlik* that was performed in coffeehouses and at the sultans' palaces has evolved into today's stand-up shows.

Although traditional theater is still offered in Turkey, more and more of today's artists are telling their stories in the movie theaters. Turkish cinema, which gained prominence in the 1970s, continues to flourish. One of Turkey's best-known directors, Yilmaz Guney, wrote and directed most of his movies from behind prison bars. (Guney was arrested following a military coup in 1970.) The films explored the themes of political oppression and censorship, ideas that are still discussed in Turkish films being produced today.

Literature

In ancient times, most stories and poems were related orally. Today, Turkish writers publish a wide range of poetry, plays, and novels. Many of these works delve into issues facing the Turkish people, including women's issues and political oppression. Writers are subject to censorship, however, and may be sent to prison or forced into exile because of their views.

THE ADVENTURES OF NASRETTIN HOCA

The art of telling stories is revered in Turkey and has been throughout history. One character, Nasrettin Hoca, is central to thousands of traditional tales. He uses humor and his quick wit to solve problems. In one popular story, Nasrettin Hoca is resting under a walnut tree. He spies a pumpkin vine growing in a nearby field and begins to wonder aloud about Allah's ways.

"Sometimes I just don't understand Allah," he reflects. "Just think, such tiny walnuts growing on such a magnificent tree, while large pumpkins sit in the field over there, nourished by delicate vines."

Just then, a walnut falls from the tree and strikes Nasrettin Hoca's bald head. He jumps to his feet and looks toward the heavens, saying, "Allah knows best. Where would I be now, had pumpkins grown on trees?"

United Arab Emirates

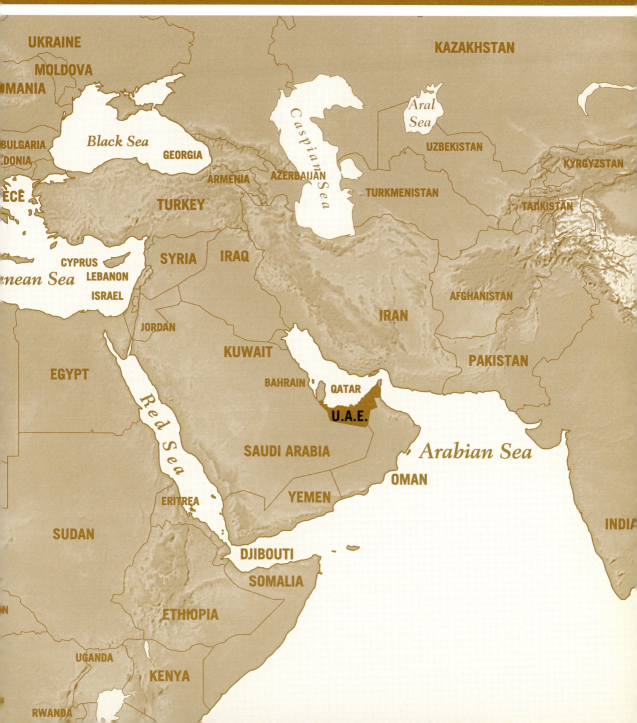

Over the past thirty years, life has changed dramatically in the United Arab Emirates (UAE). Traditionally, the Emirati—people living in the emirates—fished, farmed, or raised livestock to support their families. A nomadic lifestyle was still common in many emirates. After oil was discovered, however, the sudden wealth transformed the small country. Today, modern highways and airports facilitate travel to and around the UAE.

The Emiratis

Until the discovery of oil in 1960, fewer than 100,000 people lived in what is now the United Arab Emirates. The harsh living conditions and limited water made life very difficult. Following the discovery of oil, life changed dramatically. As construction and oil production boomed, more workers were needed, most of whom came from other countries. Today, about 88 percent of the people living in the United Arab Emirates are *expatriates,* or foreign residents.

Most Emiratis are Arabs, descended from nomadic people known as Bedouins who migrated to the region from the central and southern Arabian Peninsula. Over time, some settled in coastal villages, depending upon fishing, pearling, and trading for their income. Others maintained a nomadic lifestyle, herding their camels from one grazing ground to another.

FAST FACTS

✔ **Official name:** United Arab Emirates

✔ **Capital:** Abu Dhabi

✔ **Location:** Borders the Gulf of Oman and the Persian Gulf between Saudi Arabia and Oman

✔ **Area:** 32,000 square miles (82,880 square kilometers)

✔ **Population:** 2,484,818 (includes an estimated 1.6 million foreign residents) (July 2002 estimate)

✔ **Age distribution:**
0–14 years: 27%
15–64 years: 70%
over 65 years: 3%

✔ **Life expectancy:**
Males: 72 years
Females: 77 years

✔ **Ethnic groups:** Emirati 12%, expatriate 88% (Arab 87%, Indians and Pakistanis 9.5%, Iranians 2%, others, including Africans and Europeans, 1.5%) (estimated 1991)

✔ **Religions:** Sunni Muslim 80%, Shi'a Muslim 16%, Christian, Hindu, and other 4%

✔ **Languages:** Arabic, Persian, English, Hindi, Urdu

✔ **Currency:**
Emirati dirham (AED)
US$1 = 3.67 AED

✔ **Average annual income:** US$20,340

✔ **Major exports:** Oil, gas

Source: CIA, *The World Factbook 2002;* Library of Congress Country Study; BBC News Country Profiles.

WHAT ARE THE UNITED ARAB EMIRATES?

Six emirates (states) banded together to form the UAE in 1971. A seventh—Ras al-Khaymah—joined the federation the following year. Although the emirates share common goals, each is a distinct entity.

The largest, Abu Dhabi, stretches over 86 percent of the country. Its capital, the city of Abu Dhabi, also serves as the federal capital. Built on an island, Abu Dhabi city is connected to the mainland by two bridges. The emirate's oil reserves hold over 90 percent of the UAE's total oil. Because of this, the UAE headquarters of large oil companies are based in Abu Dhabi city.

North of Abu Dhabi is the second largest emirate, Dubai (also spelled Dubayy). Dubai has roughly 45 miles (72 kilometers) of Persian Gulf coastline. The capital, Dubai city, is the nation's largest industrial center. It is also home to Jumeirah Beach, one of the country's top tourist attractions.

Bordering Dubai on the north is the emirate of Sharjah, the third largest emirate. It is the only emirate to have coastlines on both the Persian Gulf and the Gulf of Oman, although the land on the east coast is separated from the rest of Sharjah by another emirate. Sharjah city, the capital of the emirate, is located on the Persian Gulf coast. It is widely recognized as the art center of the UAE. In 1998, Sharjah's ruler, Sheikh (SHAYK) bin Mohamed Al Qassimi, funded the "Sharjah Prize," awarded by the United Nations Educational, Scientific and Cultural Organization (UNESCO) every two years. The recipients of the prize are awarded $25,000 each in recognition of their efforts to promote Arab culture.

The smallest of the emirates, Ajman, lies on the coast within Sharjah's borders. Its coastline offers a natural harbor near the capital city of Ajman. Fishing and dhow (DOW) building have contributed greatly to the local economy for centuries, and they continue to do so today. (A dhow is a traditional Arab boat.) Ajman is also known for its beautiful white sand beaches.

North of Sharjah is the emirate of Umm al-Qaywayn. This small emirate still relies heavily on fishing and date palm cultivation. It is also well known as a center for wildlife. One of its islands, Sinaiyah, is home to the world's third largest Socotra cormorant colony. (Socotra cormorants are large birds found only in the Persian Gulf region.) Several endangered Arabian gazelles have been released on the island and are adapting well. Between the island and the mainland are sand and mud flats inhabited by a large number of water birds.

The northernmost emirate on the Persian Gulf is Ras al-Khaymah. Fertile plains extend from the coast eastward to the Hajar Mountains. Several islands are included in the Ras al-Khaymah emirate. Traditionally, agriculture and fishing were important in the region. Today, Ras al-Khaymah supplies many of the fruits and vegetables sold in the UAE.

One of the smaller emirates, Fujayrah, is the only state to be located entirely on the Gulf of Oman. The Hajar Mountains cover much of the emirate, creating a scenic backdrop to Fujayrah's beautiful beaches. Known for its excellent diving, Fujayrah is quickly becoming a favorite destination of tourists. Agriculture and fishing are still important occupations in this small emirate.

The beautiful cityscape of Dubai, set alongside the Persian Gulf coastline, is one of the most beautiful destinations in the United Arab Emirates.

In the northern emirates, some citizens trace their ancestry to India, Iran, or Pakistan. This small group is descended from the merchants and traders who came to the emirates from other countries centuries ago.

The expatriates in the UAE come from many different countries. Over 85 percent are Arabs from other Middle Eastern nations. Indians and Pakistanis are the next largest group, at 9.5 percent. Iranian nationals make up 2 percent of the population. The remaining 1.5 percent is primarily from European and African nations.

The expatriates work in all different types of jobs. Highly educated expatriates often serve as consultants for various industries or work as managers. Others are hired as domestic help, or work in factories or shops. Life can be difficult for the expatriates who work in the lower-paying jobs. Many were cheated by labor contractors who promised them jobs in the UAE that never materialized. Many came to the UAE because they could not find work in their own countries. Most have left their families behind and live as frugally as possible in order to send money back home. The expatriates who are employed in a professional capacity often enjoy a higher standard of living than in their own country, however.

Land and Resources

The arid desert that covers most of the United Arab Emirates and the searing heat of summer made life extremely difficult before the 1970s. After the UAE's most valuable resources—oil and natural gas—were discovered, however, the emirates could afford the modern conveniences that have transformed their way of life.

Geography

Located on the eastern side of the Arabian Peninsula, the United Arab Emirates borders both the Persian Gulf and the Gulf of Oman. The western tip of the UAE borders Qatar. Saudi Arabia lies to the south, while Oman adjoins the UAE on the east. The seven emirates (states) that make up the UAE cover 32,000 square miles (82,880 square kilometers), an area slightly smaller than Maine.

There are four geographical regions within the UAE: the desert, the coastal lowlands, the Hajar Mountains, and the islands. The desert region is the largest, stretching from east to west between Oman and Qatar and north to south between Dubai and Saudi Arabia. The largest dunes, blown into peaks as high as 330 feet (100 meters) by the constant winds from the northwest, are found in the southeastern part of the country.

Two oases (oh-AY-seez)—fertile green areas within a desert—are located in the desert region. The al-Liwa Oasis is in south-central Abu Dhabi. It is made up of a series of small oases that formed around wells pumping water from the underground aquifer. Date palms are commercially grown in al-Liwa. The Buraymi Oasis lies east of Abu Dhabi city, on the border of the UAE and Oman. It is also an agricultural center.

Most of the coastal lowlands region extends the length of the UAE's Persian Gulf coastline, but a narrow stretch also lines the Batinah—the eastern coast of the UAE. Along the Persian Gulf, the wide coastal plain is home to many mangrove forests. Mangrove trees have a tangle of roots that provide a protected habitat for fish. *Sabkhats,* or salt marshes, form south of Abu Dhabi city and again east of Qatar. These flat areas are devoid of life and covered with a thick layer of salt left behind when the groundwater evaporates in the desert heat. In contrast, the coastal lowlands of the Batinah are quite narrow, tucked in between the Hajar Mountains and the Gulf of Oman.

The Hajar Mountains run from north to south in the eastern UAE. Formed when the plates lying under the earth's surface shifted millions

Even though modern conveniences have made crossing the desert a possibility, the climate and conditions remain rough and forebidding.

of years ago, the mountains now tower above the sea. The tallest peak in the UAE portion of the Hajar Mountains is Jabal Yibir, which reaches 5,010 feet (1,527 meters). Although there are no permanent rivers in the UAE, deep gorges called *wadis* have been carved into the mountain slopes over the centuries. These riverbeds are usually dry, but after winter rains they carry the runoff.

The UAE claims several islands in the Persian Gulf. The country's capital city, Abu Dhabi, is built on an island. Islands also serve as collection points for offshore oil and natural gas production. Three of these islands—the Greater and Lesser Tunb Islands and Abu Musa Island—are claimed by both Iran and the UAE.

Major Cities

Most of the people in the United Arab Emirates—90 percent—live in urban areas. The cities of Abu Dhabi, Dubai, and Sharjah are the largest metropolitan areas. Abu Dhabi city serves as the capital of both the Emirate of Abu Dhabi and the UAE. Government offices are located here, as are the headquarters of many companies doing business in the UAE. Dubai city, the main port in the UAE, is the busiest commercial center in the country. Many of the country's industrial plants are located in Dubai. Sharjah city is known for its art district, where artists are supported with

Dubai city is home to the headquarters of many international companies and plays host for business conferences and annual meetings for many other companies around the world.

classes, studios, and exhibition opportunities. Most of the people living inland are clustered around the Buraymi Oasis in Abu Dhabi.

Climate

Summers in the United Arab Emirates are extremely hot and uncomfortable. Between May and October, temperatures inland often reach 120° F (49° C). The coastal regions are typically a little cooler, but high humidity levels turn the coasts into a sauna.

Winter temperatures, ranging from 68° to 95° F (20° to 35° C), provide much-needed relief. Most of the rain falls during the winter months. Abu Dhabi, with its wide expanse of desert, receives the least amount of rain—less than 2 inches (5 centimeters) each year. Ras al-Khaymah in northern UAE gets the most rain, an average of 5 inches (13 centimeters) annually.

Sandstorms, caused by strong winds known as the *shammal* and the *khamsin,* are a common hazard. The *shammal* blows from the northwest, typically in the months before and after summer. The *khamsin* blasts the UAE during the summer months. Both types of winds can create sandstorms so thick that air and highway traffic must be delayed.

Natural Resources

By far the most important resources found in the United Arab Emirates are the oil and gas reserves that have fueled the country's economy since the 1960s. Abu Dhabi was the first emirate to discover oil, and its reserves make up about 90 percent of the total reserves found in the UAE. Experts predict that the oil found in the UAE reserves will last 100 years if today's production levels are maintained.

Water is very limited in the UAE. Because of the population explosion that followed the discovery of oil, the UAE has had to invest

BARGAIN HUNTING

Each town and city has had its own *souk,* or marketplace, since early days. Typically, the souks offer a wide range of products, and the vendors of each type of product are all located near one another. For instance, gold merchants are found in the gold souk, while spice shops are in the spice souk. This arrangement makes it easy for shoppers to compare quality and prices—and find a bargain. In small towns, the souk was often set up only one day a week. Today, although modern stores and malls are found in the large cities, traditional souks still draw many shoppers.

in *desalination* plants that remove the salt from seawater to produce drinking water. By 1985, the nation depended upon twenty-two desalination plants to produce enough drinking water. The desalination plants often have power stations attached that generate electricity.

Plants and Animals

The large areas of sandy desert found in the UAE do not provide a hospitable environment for many plants or animals. After winter rains, however, some grasses appear for a short time. Along the coasts and around the oases, native palm, acacia, and tamarisk trees flourish. A wide variety of plants—from fruits and vegetables to ornamental plants—grow in irrigated areas, which include the urban areas as well as the oases.

Did You Know?

Archaeologists have found evidence that camels were domesticated in the UAE at least 4,000 years ago.

Most animals seen today in the UAE are birds, including numerous species of waterfowl found along the coast. Most large mammals, including the desert oryx and the Arabian gazelle, are endangered after being hunted almost to extinction. Wildlife refuge programs have been implemented in the UAE to preserve the species that remain.

History

Ancient Days

Much of the ancient history of the United Arab Emirates is still hidden beneath sand and dirt, waiting to be discovered. The archaeological excavations that have taken place reveal evidence of people living in the region as far back as 6000 B.C.E. Farming, fishing, and copper work were part of their daily life. Fragments of Mesopotamian pottery found in ancient tombs indicate links between the ancient traders and the people living on the peninsula around 3000 B.C.E.

Trade became increasingly important at the end of the first millennium B.C.E. The discovery of a large settlement in Sharjah confirmed that traders from present-day Iran, Iraq, Greece, Saudi Arabia, and Bahrain were active in the region during this period. The wealth generated by these trading centers attracted the attention of the Achaemenid (uh-KEE-muh-nuhd) Empire of Persia (present-day Iran). From the sixth to the fourth centuries B.C.E., the Achaemenids controlled much of the Persian Gulf coast.

IMPORTANT EVENTS IN THE UNITED ARAB EMIRATES' HISTORY

6000 B.C.E.	Ancient people settle in the Hajar Mountain region.
3000 B.C.E.	Mesopotamians trade with people living in the Persian Gulf coastal areas.
6th–4th century B.C.E.	The Achaemenid (Persian) Empire controls coastal trading centers.
1st century C.E.	The northern city of ad-Dour gains prominence as a religious and commercial center.
200	Arabs from present-day Saudi Arabia and Yemen migrate into the region. The Sassanian (Persian) Empire conquers the coastal areas, remaining in control for four centuries.
610	Mohammad introduces the new religion of Islam in the holy city of Mecca.
630	Islam spreads throughout the Arabian Peninsula.
1507	The Portuguese arrive in the Persian Gulf and take control of the Strait of Hormuz.
1600	The British establish trading posts in India and use the Persian Gulf to ship goods back home.
1622	Tired of the Portuguese obstructing passage through the Persian Gulf, the British attack and take the fort overlooking the Strait of Hormuz.
1761	The Bani Yas tribe discovers a freshwater well on Abu Dhabi Island.
1793	The al-Nahyan family, rulers of the Bani Yas, moves to Abu Dhabi Island and builds a fort around the well.
1798	The British sign a treaty with the Al Bu Said family, the main rival of the Qawasim. The Qawasim begin attacking British ships in the Persian Gulf.
1819	The British demolish the Qawasim fleet and take control of Ras al-Khaymah.

1820	Britain signs a truce with the rulers of the Persian Gulf states, thereafter called the Trucial States.
1833	The Al Bu Falasah family of the Bani Yas tribe settles in Dubai.
1892	The Trucial States sign a treaty with Britain to become protectorates. Britain gains the right to control the states' foreign policy.
1930	The pearling industry collapses due to the introduction of cultured pearls. Poverty becomes a major problem in the emirates.
1939	Oil companies explore for oil in Abu Dhabi.
1960	Oil companies discover an offshore oil reserve in Abu Dhabi.
1966	Sheikh Zayed bin Sultan al-Nahyan becomes leader of Abu Dhabi.
1968	Britain announces plans to leave the Persian Gulf region by 1971.
1971	The United Arab Emirates proclaims its status as a sovereign nation, with six member emirates.
1972	Ras al-Khaymah joins the UAE.
1990	Iraq invades Kuwait, starting the Persian Gulf War. The UAE joins the international coalition fighting against Iraq.
2000	Abu Dhabi TV begins satellite broadcasts. The emirate of Dubai founds an Internet City to promote telecommunications services and Internet programming.
2001	The emirate of Dubai establishes Dubai Media City to encourage international media companies to set up headquarters in the emirate.

The coastal city of ad-Dour in today's emirate of Umm al-Qaywayn rose to prominence during the early years of the first century C.E. One of the main attractions was the temple dedicated to Shams, a sun god. The city also enjoyed a reputation as a commercial center whose merchants and traders handled goods from as far away as China.

Arabs from present-day Saudi Arabia and Yemen migrated into the present-day UAE territory between 200 and 600 C.E. Some were traders; others settled in the coastal region and relied upon fishing. The nomadic tribes herded their camels and goats through the desert. These tribes jealously guarded any water sources they discovered, often building forts around the wells and springs.

The Persians also returned to the area during the third century C.E., this time as the Sassanian (suh-SAY-nee-uhn) Empire. Once again, they gained control of coastal trading centers. Their rule lasted until the seventh century.

The Arrival of Islam

In 610, according to Islamic tradition, the Prophet Mohammad received revelations from Allah, or God, concerning the way people should behave in their relationships with Allah and with each other. Mohammad began to preach about Islam, which literally means "submission."

As the number of converts grew, Muslim armies spread the new religion throughout Arabia, including the present-day emirates. The tribes they defeated swore loyalty to Mohammad and converted to Islam.

The port city of Julfar in present-day Ras al-Khaymah became a great commercial center in the seventh century. Its merchants sailed east to Asia, trading with China, India, Vietnam, and Sri Lanka. They also headed south around the tip of the Arabian Peninsula to trade in East Africa.

Contacts with Europeans

The Portuguese were the first Europeans to arrive in the Persian Gulf region. The variety of luxurious goods for sale convinced the Portuguese that they needed to control the Strait of Hormuz, the narrow waterway connecting the Persian Gulf with the Gulf of Oman. Control of the shipping lane would give them control over the trade routes and the ships that used them. In 1507, the Portuguese captured the fortress overlooking the Strait of Hormuz. From there, they controlled the sea trade in the Persian Gulf for over a century.

The Portuguese were harsh rulers. People living in the region were forced to pay heavy taxes. Anyone who spoke out or otherwise challenged the Portuguese was thrown into prison or punished severely.

By the early seventeenth century, British and Dutch traders had established posts in the Persian Gulf region. At first the British East India Company concentrated on India, shipping goods by sea through the Persian Gulf, then overland to the Mediterranean. The Portuguese didn't want any other powers in the area, however, and they harassed British ships that sailed through the Gulf. Finally, in 1622, Britain attacked the Portuguese and gained control of the Strait of Hormuz. Still primarily concerned with shipping goods from India to Britain, the British virtually ignored the inland region.

The Bani Yas and the Qawasim

One of the most influential tribes in the history of the United Arab Emirates, the Bani Yas were based in al-Liwa Oasis. Their tribal lands included the present-day emirates of Abu Dhabi and Dubai. Although the Bani Yas families ranged over large areas looking for grazing and water for their camels and goats during much of the year, they gathered at al-Liwa Oasis during the hottest months. There they cultivated groves of date palms.

In 1761, the Bani Yas discovered a large freshwater well on what is now Abu Dhabi Island. By 1793, the al-Nahyans—the rulers of the Bani Yas tribe—had relocated to the island. There they built a fort around the well. Pearling and the cultivation of date palms provided income for the al-Nahyans.

Another branch of the Bani Yas, the Al Bu Falasah family, settled in present-day Dubai in 1833. Because of its location and deep port, Dubai quickly became an important center of trade.

The northern ports of Sharjah and Ras al-Khaymah were ruled by a tribe called the Qawasim. They were skilled seafarers, with more than sixty ships and 20,000 sailors. The Qawasim had little to do with the Bani Yas because they were not competing for the same territory. Instead, the Qawasim vied with the British and the Al Bu Saids of Oman for control of the Persian Gulf.

In 1798, the British and the Al Bu Saids agreed not to attack each other's ships. The Qawasim believed that the British, now cooperating

Did You Know?

The fort built by the al-Nahyan family on Abu Dhabi Island is one of the oldest forts still in existence in the UAE. Known as al-Husn, the White Fort, the historical site is a favorite tourist destination today.

with the Qawasim's main adversary, the Al Bu Saids, had become an enemy of the Qawasim as well. They began attacking British ships. The British viewed the Qawasim as pirates because of the attacks. Finally, in 1819, the British fired on the Qawasim ships anchored at Ras al-Khaymah and sank or captured the entire fleet.

The Trucial States

In 1820, Britain forced the sheikhs in the lower Persian Gulf to sign a truce designed to maintain peace in the region. Other treaties followed, and the coastal areas soon became known as the Trucial States. In 1892, the states became *protectorates* of Britain. This meant that Britain would defend and protect the sheikhdoms in return for having control over all foreign relations.

The Discovery of Oil

Although Britain controlled the foreign policy of the Trucial States, it had little to do with local affairs. When the pearling industry collapsed in the 1930s, intense poverty became a big problem in many of the sheikhdoms. The ruler of Abu Dhabi, Sheikh Shakhbut al-Nahyan,

United Arab Emirates Supreme Council president Sheikh Zayed bin Sultan al-Nahyan has forged strong business and political ties with the United States.

invited an oil company to explore for oil in 1939. When nothing was found, he allowed another company to search offshore. In 1960, the first oil reserve in the present-day emirates was discovered. Abu Dhabi's vast reserves began to produce unbelievable wealth for the desert sheikhdom.

In 1966, Sheikh Zayed bin Sultan al-Nahyan was named ruler of Abu Dhabi. He used the new money to modernize the emirate, building hospitals and medical clinics, schools, roads, and airports. Some of the oil windfall was shared with the other sheikhdoms.

In 1968, Britain made a surprising announcement: it was planning to withdraw from the Persian Gulf region in 1971. Six gulf rulers agreed to form a federation that would be called the United Arab Emirates. (Bahrain and Qatar originally considered joining the federation, but ultimately decided to remain independent.) On December 2, 1971, the United Arab Emirates was officially established. A year later, Ras al-Khaymah joined the UAE, bringing the number of emirates to seven.

The United Arab Emirates Today

Sheikh Zayed bin Sultan al-Nahyan has served as president of the UAE since its founding. His strong leadership and support for religious tolerance, women's rights, and shared wealth have won him the praise and respect of international leaders as well as of the Emiratis.

In 1991, the UAE joined the United States and other countries in fighting the Persian Gulf War. Emiratis also took part in the rebuilding effort in Kuwait once Iraq was forced to withdraw.

Economy

Once dependent upon agriculture, livestock, fishing, and pearling, the United Arab Emirates is today one of the world's wealthiest countries due to its extensive oil reserves. Although oil and natural gas generate enough revenues to support the country, the government has worked hard to develop a diversified economy. This is important, since annual oil income varies widely based on oil prices and worldwide consumption levels. Today, banking, manufacturing, and real estate have become important economic sectors. Traditional occupations such as agriculture and fishing continue as a source of income in the UAE as well.

Business and Industry

The United Arab Emirates offers many incentives to businesses that locate there. The lack of taxes lures many industries, as does the strategic location near major shipping lanes. Many workers, most of them from other countries, are available to work at relatively low wages.

Because of the small native population and the booming economy, most of the workforce are citizens of other countries. The majority of foreign workers arrived during the 1970s and 1980s. Most come from other Arab countries, although many Indians, Pakistanis, and Iranians also work in the UAE. Professionals and those in managerial positions are typically offered a contract before they arrive in the country. They command good salaries and employment benefits and enjoy a high standard of living. Unskilled or semiskilled laborers are not always so fortunate. While most are able to find legitimate jobs in safe working conditions, others end up working long hours for low pay in unregulated industries. It is against the law in the UAE to form a union, strike, or bargain collectively.

Most high-level government posts are filled by Emirati citizens, both men and women. Most women work in the education and health ministries. Although women have been able to pursue careers outside the home since the UAE was established, many conservative Emiratis still believe that women should not work for pay. This is especially true if their jobs would put women into contact with men.

A visitor stops by a booth to review company information at GITEX 2003, the Gulf Information and Technology Exhibition in Dubai. Attracting 82,000 visitors, GITEX has helped the government turn the emirate of Dubai into the information and technology center of the Middle East.

Oil and Gas

The oil and gas industries of the UAE produce most of the country's income. After oil was discovered in Abu Dhabi in 1960, building the infrastructure needed to produce and export the oil became a massive undertaking. Not only did the oil fields need to be developed, pipelines and ports had to be built. Housing for the thousands of workers needed by the industry had to be constructed.

At the time oil was discovered in Abu Dhabi, the emirates were still separate entities under British control. Therefore, all the oil revenue was controlled by Abu Dhabi's emir. It was used locally to spur development in Abu Dhabi. The same was true for Dubai, which began receiving oil revenues in 1970. After the UAE was founded in 1971, oil revenues were shared throughout the nation. Much of the money was spent to develop the UAE's infrastructure: airports, highways, ports, electrical power plants, and communications systems.

The UAE is a member of the Organization of Petroleum Exporting Countries (OPEC). The eleven members of OPEC meet periodically to determine how much oil each country will produce. When world oil prices drop too low, OPEC limits the amount of oil that is exported. If the prices rise too high and consumption drops, production levels are increased.

Did You Know?

Following Iraq's invasion of Kuwait in 1990, OPEC lifted production quotas so that member countries could supply the oil that Iraq and Kuwait would have exported. In 1991, the UAE alone earned $14 billion in oil revenues.

LIQUID GOLD

Only four of the seven emirates in the UAE have oil and gas reserves: Abu Dhabi, Dubai, Sharjah, and Ras al-Khaymah. Each emirate controls the exploration and exploitation of its oil and gas reserves.

Petroleum engineers began exploring for oil in Abu Dhabi in 1939. The first field was discovered in 1960, and three years later, oil revenues began to change the way of life in the emirate. The reserves found in Abu Dhabi are the country's largest; they hold about 90 percent of the UAE's estimated 98 billion barrels of oil.

The search for oil in Dubai began in 1937, but it wasn't until 1966 that the first offshore field was located. Dubai's reserves are small in comparison to those in Abu Dhabi. They are expected to run out by 2016 if current levels of production continue.

Sharjah has a small offshore oil reserve—discovered in 1973—that it shares with Iran, Umm al-Qaywayn, and Ajman. A larger, inland field was discovered in 1980.

Ras al-Khaymah has the smallest reserves of any of the oil-producing emirates. Production began in the early 1980s; most of the revenues are being used to fund further exploration.

Although most members abide by the production limits imposed by OPEC, compliance is voluntary. Since the 1980s, Dubai has regularly produced and exported more than its quota. Because its reserves are relatively small, emirate officials believed that it was more efficient to operate the fields at or near capacity. Beginning in the late 1980s, Abu Dhabi has periodically ignored OPEC limits. It argues that the OPEC quotas are artificially low in comparison to those for other countries whose reserves are the same size as Abu Dhabi's.

Industries

Both the United Arab Emirates government and local leaders have made concerted efforts to attract new industry to the country. However, there is little coordination between the various groups, so resources are often squandered. For example, nine cement factories regularly produce four times the amount of cement that is needed locally. The same situation occurs in the steel, plastics, and food industries.

THE PEARLING INDUSTRY

Before the 1930s, some of the wealthiest people in the emirates were the pearl merchants. In addition, thousands of men supported their families by working in the pearling industry during the four-month pearling season. Boats carried divers to the oyster beds off the coast of the emirates, where each diver made about fifty dives a day. After clipping their noses shut with special clasps, they hung a special net around their necks and dove to the ocean floor. A rope connected each diver to a person on board the ship. Underwater, the diver collected oysters in the net, always remaining alert for dangers such as sharks and poisonous snakes. When a diver needed a breath or had filled the net, he tugged on the rope and was hauled to the surface. At the end of the day, the men opened the oysters they had collected and removed any pearls that they found. The pearls were sold in the souk at the end of the voyage, and the profits were shared among the crew.

The pearling industry collapsed in the 1930s when Japan introduced cultured (mass-produced) pearls into the world market. Many men who had relied upon pearling for income migrated to Kuwait, Bahrain, Qatar, and Saudi Arabia to work in the newly established oil industries.

One of the few new architectural references to the past, this hotel in Dubai is built to resemble a dhow, a traditional fishing and pearling boat.

About 80 percent of the UAE's factories are based in Abu Dhabi, Dubai, and Sharjah. Dubai is considered the industrial center of the UAE, and many multinational companies operate there, including Mitsubishi, Minnesota Mining and Manufacturing (3M), Union Carbide, and Xerox. Most of the textile firms are owned by Indian companies. Dubai is also known for its dry-dock facility, one of the largest in the Persian Gulf, where tankers and other large seagoing vessels can be repaired and maintained.

Agriculture

Although farming in the oases has been practiced since ancient times, it doesn't contribute a great deal to the modern economy. Agricultural production has increased in recent decades, but nearly three-fourths of the food eaten in the United Arab Emirates is still imported from other countries.

Lack of water is the primary obstacle to farming in the UAE, although pests such as locusts and the extreme summer heat also cause difficulties. Using oil revenues, the government has supported the development of new irrigation systems in order to increase the amount of land being farmed. While these efforts have been successful in the short term, the long-term effects are problematic. Underground aquifers are being emptied, resulting in increased levels of salt in the soil and remaining water.

Date palms are the most widely cultivated plant in the UAE. The largest groves are found in al-Liwa Oasis in southern Abu Dhabi. Citrus and mangoes are also grown commercially in the UAE. Vegetable crops include tomatoes, cabbage, eggplant, squash, and cauliflower. Most vegetables are grown in Ras al-Khaymah.

In addition to vegetables and fruits, farmers in the UAE raise poultry for consumption and for egg production. Dairy products continue to be an important part of the Emirati diet as well, and dairy farms produce nearly all the milk consumed in the UAE. Traditionally, camel's milk was most important in the emirates, although sheep's and goat's milk was also consumed. Dairy cows were much rarer, although some families in the coastal regions did raise them. Today, most commercial dairy farmers raise milk cows and goats, though many Emiratis still keep a camel in their family compound to provide milk.

Fishing once provided a major source of income for Emirati families. Today, the UAE government heavily subsidizes fishermen who use traditional fishing methods, financing half the cost of boats and equipment and maintaining or repairing the boats for free. As a result, the number of fishermen more than doubled between 1980 and 1990. Today, nearly all of the fish consumed in the UAE is caught locally or raised on fish farms in Umm al-Qaywayn. Dried fish is an important export.

Media and Communications

Over the past few decades, the United Arab Emirates has established a modern communications system linking the populated areas of the country. Television and radio broadcasts are widely available.

In 2001, Dubai founded Dubai Media City—acres of office buildings, production facilities, and living quarters—to encourage international media companies to establish outlets in the emirate. One of the major attractions is the low cost of operations. Freedom of speech, unusual in many Middle Eastern countries, is also guaranteed under the UAE constitution. To date, several major organizations— including Reuters, CNN Arabic, and Saudi-owned Middle East Broadcasting Center—have established offices in Dubai Media City.

Abu Dhabi TV, launched in 2000, is a satellite broadcasting company based in the emirate of Abu Dhabi. Originally offering a variety of political talk shows, sitcoms, game shows, and news programming, Abu Dhabi TV gained prominence in 2003 when it began offering in-depth, twenty-four-hour coverage of the war in Iraq.

Many of UAE's citizens are avid Internet users. Dubai has taken the lead in this area as well, establishing an Internet City in 2000 to capitalize on the growing interest in telecommunications services and Internet programming. The UAE government, as the main provider of Internet services, routinely blocks certain political sites as well as those it finds morally offensive.

Religion and Beliefs

Islam has been an integral part of life for people living in the Arabian Peninsula since its introduction in the seventh century. The people living in what is now the United Arab Emirates were among the first to adopt the new religion. Today, nearly all Emiratis are Sunni Muslims. A small group of Sunnis living in al-Buraymi Oasis belong to the strict

Wahhabi sect. (Wahhabism is the variety of Islam current in Saudi Arabia. Its followers accept a very narrow view of Islam, rejecting any beliefs different from their own.)

The UAE constitution guarantees freedom of religion, as long as non-Muslims do not attempt to convert Muslims to other religions. The expatriates living in the UAE are primarily Sunni and Shi'ite Muslims. A small number of expatriates follow Christian or Hindu traditions. The largest concentration of Christian churches and schools is in Abu Dhabi and Dubai.

Islam

All Muslims follow the teachings of the Prophet Mohammad, who established Islam in the seventh century. They believe in one God—Allah—who revealed the Qur'an, the Muslim holy book (commonly known in the West as the Koran) to Mohammad. According to Islamic tradition, Mohammad is the last in a series of prophets that includes Abraham (patriarch of the Jews) and Jesus (founder of Christianity). (To learn more about Islam, see pages ix–xii in the introduction to this volume.)

Everyday Life

Life in the United Arab Emirates today is very different from the traditional lifestyles that were still the norm forty years ago. The sudden wealth from oil exports has improved education, health care, and general living standards. Today, the cities of the UAE offer amenities found in any modern country.

Family Life

For centuries, families in the United Arab Emirates region have been guided by Islam and the ancient tribal culture of their ancestors. One

HERITAGE CENTERS

Because life has changed so quickly in the United Arab Emirates, the government has established heritage centers and museums throughout the country in an effort to preserve the past. In Abu Dhabi's Heritage Village, for example, visitors can wander through a replica of a Bedouin encampment, ride a camel, watch a falconry demonstration, and visit a traditional souk. In other cities, heritage centers offer the opportunity to see traditional folk dances or watch dhows being built.

important tenet of Arab tribal culture is the importance of family. Loyalty to one's family means that family considerations take precedence over everything else, including work or one's own desires. Decisions are made based on what is best for the family, not for any one individual member. People are very careful not to do or say anything that would bring dishonor to their family. This sense of loyalty and honor extends beyond one's immediate family to include the clan (a large group of related families) and the tribe (a group of related clans).

The extended family is common in the UAE, with up to four generations sharing a family compound. This arrangement enables family members to share the work of caring for children, the sick, and the elderly. The oldest man in the family makes the decisions about issues affecting the family, usually after listening to the opinions of other male family members. Although other aspects of life in the UAE have undergone rapid changes, the traditional family structure provides a needed stability.

Most Emiratis follow clearly defined, traditional roles. Men are the head of the family, the decision makers and providers. Women care for the family and the home. In rural areas, women also help with the livestock and farming. Children are expected to obey their parents and show respect to their elders. After 1960, more opportunities became available for women to work outside the home. President Sheikh Zayed bin Sultan al-Nahyan has been a strong supporter of women's rights since the federation was established in 1971, ensuring that educational and employment opportunities are available to women.

Traditionally, Emirati marriages were arranged by the families of the bride and groom. Family connections were one of the most important considerations. Ideally, a man would marry his cousin, the daughter of his father's brother. Today, although social connections are still important, most families take their children's opinions into account when selecting a spouse for them.

Once a man has agreed to his family's choice for a bride, he must get permission from her father. A bride-price is agreed upon, and a marriage contract is signed. At that point, a couple is legally married. However, the two don't live together as husband and wife until after the wedding ceremony. The bride's preparation for the wedding ceremony traditionally lasts forty days. During this time, only her family may see her. The week before the wedding is filled with celebrations—segregated by gender—

that include feasts, traditional music, singing, and dancing. When the bride and groom are from wealthy families, the celebrations get quite elaborate and may even include camel races and public concerts. A few days before the wedding, all the women join the bride for *Laylat al-Henna* (the night of the henna). The bride's hands and feet are decorated with intricate patterns using henna, a plant-based dye.

In recent years, as Emirati women have become more educated, some have chosen to complete their education and pursue a career before getting married. A few have elected not to marry at all.

Dress

Most Emirati men and women still wear traditional clothing today. Women's clothing is typically made from bright, colorful fabrics. Reds, yellows, greens, and blues are especially popular, both as solids and in patterns. The clothes are made from a wide range of fabrics including cottons, silks, satins, and chiffons. Designs are often embroidered on the garments in gold or silver thread.

Women wear a full-length dress called a *dara'a*, which is generally embroidered around the neck and wrists. On special occasions, a light

Young women in festive attire prepare for a ceremony to welcome United Arab Emirates President Sheik Zayed in Dubai. An occasion such as this calls for women to wear their most important headpieces and finest dresses.

dress called a *thawb* is layered over the *dara'a*. Special *thawbs* are worn for Eid celebrations or during weddings. The *sirwal*—loose-fitting trousers—is worn under the *dara'a*. When women appear in public, they don an *abaya*—a full-length black cloak—and a *shaileh*—a black veil wrapped around the head. Sometimes the veil is used to cover the face, but more often, the traditional *burgu* is worn. The *burgu* covers only part of the face, allowing the eyes, cheeks, and chin to be seen.

Jewelry is also an important part of the Emirati woman's attire. Earrings, necklaces, and anklets made of gold and silver and set with precious stones are worn for special occasions. Headpieces crafted from gold hold dangling strings of coins that fall the length of the woman's hair. Young girls often wear traditional bracelets that are attached to five rings—one for each finger.

The *dishdasha*, or *kandura*, is the ankle-length, loose-fitting garment worn by most Emirati men. These garments were traditionally made of cotton, although today's fabrics are generally a blend of cotton and synthetics. The dishdasha is usually white, although dark colors are sometimes seen. Traditional headpieces are made of three parts: the *gahfiyya*, or skullcap worn directly on the head; the *ghutra*, a solid white or red checked cloth; and the *agal*—a twisted black cord made of wool—that holds the *gahfiyya* and *ghutra* in place. (Religious scholars usually wear a white *agal*.)

On special occasions, a sleeveless cloak called a *bisht* is worn over the dishdasha. These cloaks may be black or beige, and they are often trimmed in gold.

Education

At the beginning of the twentieth century, none of the emirates had a formal education system. Some boys attended religious schools where they learned to recite from the Qur'an. Others attended schools founded by the pearl merchants in Abu Dhabi, Dubai, and Sharjah. Britain opened the first school to offer a comprehensive education in 1953. This school was for boys only, but a girls' school opened soon after. Beginning in the late 1950s, Kuwait and other Persian Gulf countries used some of their oil revenues to build schools in the emirates. They supported the schools until the emirates were able to do so themselves in the 1960s and 1970s.

Since the founding of the United Arab Emirates in 1971, education has been a top priority. Children ages six to twelve are required to attend school. Those who wish to continue their education may attend secondary school for six years, followed by university. Education is free for all Emirati, from primary school through university. This includes texts, school uniforms, and transportation. Anyone who wants to continue with postgraduate work must study abroad, and the government finances these efforts as well. Students who complete a university-level education receive a financial award from the government. Although education is provided for everyone, schools are segregated by gender.

All villages have a primary school. Secondary schools have been established in larger towns, and each has boarding facilities for children who don't live nearby. Great strides have been made in improving the literacy rates in the UAE. In the late 1970s, less than 25 percent of the population could read and write. Within two decades, literacy rates had risen to 80 percent. Women in particular have taken advantage of educational opportunities. Today, women outnumber men at the university level.

Recreation and Leisure

Many traditional Arab pastimes are still enjoyed in the United Arab Emirates. One of the most popular is camel racing. While the races were once cross-country, today there are racetracks built especially for camel races. Races featuring Arabian horses also draw large crowds. The Dubai World Cup offers one of the richest purses of any horse race in the world. Both camel and horse owners spend a great deal of time pampering and training their animals.

Falconry, the sport of hunting with a trained bird of prey, is very popular in the UAE. Much time is spent training the falcons to hunt bustards and other desert birds. It is a very expensive hobby, so only a wealthy few participate. During hunts, the falcon tracks down its prey, often covering 3 miles (5 kilometers) before the chase ends. Many falconers follow the hunt from horseback or in an open truck.

In the coastal areas, boat races test the skills of sailors. The sailboats are modeled after the traditional dhow that has been used in Arabia for centuries. Yacht races and powerboat competitions are gaining popularity.

Modern sports are quite popular in the UAE as well. Of these, soccer (known as football in the UAE) has the most fans. Each town has its own team, as do the schools from primary level through college.

Competitions are held on the local, regional, and national levels. Cricket and rugby, bowling, tennis, and golf are also popular.

One annual event that draws a lot of attention is the UAE Desert Challenge car rally. Drivers from around the world race cars, trucks, and motorcycles through the deserts of the UAE. The five-day event tests drivers and mechanics as they battle to complete the course without getting stuck in the sand dunes.

Children have access to museums and activity parks. Sharjah's science museum and Discovery Center offer interactive exhibits. Traditional games such as *al-Meryeihana,* a skipping game for girls, and *al-Ghomaid,* a game similar to blindman's buff, are still enjoyed in many areas, although Emirati children are just as fascinated by video games and television programs as their counterparts in the West.

Food

As in many countries in the Persian Gulf, the cuisine of the United Arab Emirates reflects the Arab heritage of its people as well as the international influence of the foreigners who have lived and worked in the region since ancient times. Traders from Persia (present-day Iran) and India introduced spices and cooking techniques from those regions into the area.

Today, traditional Arab and Middle Eastern foods are readily available in the UAE. Street vendors offer tasty treats such as *shawarma,* roasted meats that are sliced thinly and served in pita bread. *Shisha*

MURABYAN (SHRIMP ABU DHABI)

This dish features the pink Gulf shrimp that are caught off the coast of the United Arab Emirates. It can be served by itself or with rice.

1 pound large shrimp or prawns (about 12)
  Salt, to taste
1/2 cup all-purpose flour
2 tablespoons butter or margarine
2 tablespoons olive oil
1 large onion, chopped
2 garlic cloves, minced
2 tablespoons chopped cilantro
Juice of 1 lime (3 tablespoons)
Cilantro sprigs for garnish

Clean shrimp, removing the shell but leaving the tails intact. Sprinkle shrimp with salt. Roll lightly in flour, shaking off excess. Melt butter or margarine with olive oil in a large skillet. Add onion and garlic. Sauté until onion is tender. Add shrimp and chopped cilantro to the skillet, and sauté until shrimp are golden, about 7 minutes. Place shrimp and onions on a platter and sprinkle with lime juice. Garnish with cilantro.

Makes 4 servings.

Source: Adapted from *Mideast & Mediterranean Cuisines* by Rose Dosti.

cafés are popular gathering places for men. They discuss the latest news over a coffee or tea and smoke a *shisha*—a water pipe that is also known as a hubble-bubble pipe. Restaurants feature a variety of international cuisines, including Asian, Indian, Pakistani, Persian, and European. American fast food chains are ubiquitous in the large cities.

The main meal of the day is served at lunch. It begins with *meze* (MAY-zay), or appetizers. Several different types of meze are offered at each meal. Favorites include *hummus*, a dip made with chickpeas; *tabbouleh*, a salad made with cracked wheat, spices, and vegetables; and cheese.

The meze are followed by the main dish, which usually includes meat or seafood and grains. Lamb and chicken are eaten regularly, but pork is never served since it is prohibited by Islamic law. Since the UAE has 819 miles (1,320 kilometers) of coastline, it's not surprising to find that fish and seafood are a major part of the Emirati diet. Lobster, crab, shrimp, grouper, tuna, kingfish, and red snapper are all readily available. Traditionally, flat bread is used to scoop up the food in place of utensils.

Gahwah, or coffee, is served after meals, along with a sweet dessert. Arab coffee is typically brewed with cardamom or cloves and served without sugar or cream. Tea and fruit juices are also popular beverages. *Laban*, a mix of yogurt, water, and garlic, is a traditional Arab beverage that is still enjoyed today. Islam forbids the consumption of alcohol, although restaurants associated with hotels that cater to foreigners are allowed to sell alcohol.

A traditional Bedouin feast features *mansaf*, a dish that takes its name from the Arabic word meaning "large tray." The trays used to serve *mansaf* can measure more than six feet (1.8 meters) in diameter, and owning a large tray is considered an honor since it indicates an individual's generosity. *Mansaf* is generally served on special occasions, such as a wedding or banquet.

To make *mansaf*, a whole lamb is seasoned with herbs and cooked for hours in a yogurt sauce. The serving tray is covered with flatbread, and rice is heaped on top of the bread. The stewed lamb is then dished over the rice, and almonds or pine nuts are sprinkled on top.

Did You Know?

Cooks in the UAE use a wide variety of spices. They can find the freshest spices in the *atarineh,* or spice street, in the local *souk,* or market. A favorite spice mix includes cinnamon, cayenne pepper, and paprika. Each purchase is wrapped in paper cones known as *dukkahs.* Sesame oil, nuts, and parsley are other common ingredients in Emirati dishes.

Traditionally, guests eat communally from the tray by scooping up bites of *mansaf* with a piece of bread held in their right hands.

Holidays and Festivals

Because the United Arab Emirates is an Islamic country, its major holidays are religious in nature. Because Islam follows a lunar calendar, the dates for the festivals vary from year to year.

Ramadan, the ninth month of the Islamic year, is a time for Muslims to show their devotion to God. Although it is not technically a holiday, it is a joyous time of the year when Muslims demonstrate their obedience to Allah. During Ramadan, Muslims fast between sunrise and sunset. Food, drink, and other activities, such as smoking, are prohibited during the day. This discipline encourages compassion for the less fortunate. As the sun sets each evening, families gather for a special meal, called *iftar*, that breaks the fast. They often stay up late into the night visiting.

Eid al-Fitr is one of the biggest celebrations of the year. When the sun sets on the last day of Ramadan, a three-day period of feasting and visiting begins. Everyone gets new clothes to celebrate the occasion, and children receive gifts of money and candy from relatives.

During the month of Ramadan, many people feast and celebrate the end of the fasting day in luxurious tents set up in front of their modern homes.

Eid al-Adha, the Feast of the Sacrifice, is another major Islamic holiday. This three-day celebration occurs during the *hajj,* the time when devout Muslims make a pilgrimage to the holy city of Mecca. It commemorates the willingness of Abraham to obey God and sacrifice his son. Because of Abraham's obedience, God allowed him to sacrifice a lamb in place of the child. In preparation for Eid al-Adha, families purchase a sheep to cook for a feast. One-third of the meat is given to the poor, one-third is shared among relatives, and the family prepares the remaining third for the feast.

In addition to Eid al-Fitr and Eid al-Adha, most Muslims in the UAE observe Mohammad's birthday and the Islamic New Year. The Wahhabis do not celebrate these two occasions, since they were not observed during Mohammad's lifetime.

National Day is celebrated on December 2. It commemorates the establishment of the United Arab Emirates in 1971.

The Arts

Women have taken the lead in preserving and expanding the arts in the United Arab Emirates. Shops such as the Women's Handicraft Center in Abu Dhabi help women market their handmade goods. In some of these shops, women can demonstrate traditional crafts such as weaving.

The Sharjah Art Center has earned a reputation as the premier fine arts advocate in the UAE. Art classes for all ages and abilities are offered at the Sharjah Art Center. Traditional homes in the area have been renovated to provide working spaces for artists. The Sharjah Art Museum, built in 1997, is the largest art museum in the Persian Gulf region. It has thirty-two exhibition halls that feature both local and international shows.

Because nearly all Emirati are Muslims, they follow Islamic guidelines in creating art. Since the Qur'an prohibits the drawing of humans and animals, calligraphy—beautiful writing—has become one of the premier Islamic arts. Many items are decorated with calligraphy, including the decorative tiles used to adorn mosques. Geometric patterns called *arabesque* are also typical of Islamic art. These are worked into rugs and wall hangings and used to decorate pottery and other objects.

Music has played a vital role in many aspects of Emirati life. Many of the traditional songs are related to a specific chore or task, such as drawing water from the well. During the pearling days, a *nahham*—a song leader—would be hired for each boat. With a song for each task, such as setting sail or approaching the oyster beds, he would lead the men through their work.

Traditional dances such as the *ayyalah* reenact legendary battles. Swords, rifles, and sticks are often an integral part of the dances, which are performed to traditional music. Instruments include the *tamboura,* a relative of the harp; the *manior,* a percussion instrument worn around the waist which makes a clicking sound as the musician moves; and drums.

Storytelling and poetry are highly valued in the UAE. In the not-so-distant past, nomads gathered around their fires each night and took turns entertaining one another with stories, legends, and poetry. Not every poem was strictly for entertainment. Some were told in order to pass down the shared history of the tribe and information about tribal territories, including the location of grazing grounds and watering spots. The oral literature of the UAE includes a collection of folklore, proverbs, and parables as well.

Yemen

Yemen lies on the southwestern tip of the Arabian Peninsula. It is bordered on the north by Saudi Arabia and Oman on the northeast. Southeast of Yemen is the Gulf of Aden, which leads to the Indian Ocean and the Arabia Sea. The Red Sea borders the eastern coastline. Yemen also includes approximately 112 islands. The total area of Yemen is slightly less than that of Texas.

Yemen was once divided into the Yemen Arab Republic and the People's Democratic Republic of Yemen. In 1990, these two countries merged to form the Republic of Yemen. This Arabic-speaking country is considered one of the poorest nations in the world.

The Yemenis

With a population of over 19 million, Yemen is the most populated area on the Arabian Peninsula. About 90 percent of Yemenis are Arabs. The rest are Pakistanis, Somalis, and Indians. Most Somalis in Yemen arrived as refugees fleeing from chaos and civil war in their country. The Indian population is attributed to economic and political ties that date back over two millennia.

Traditionally, most Yemenis have lived on farms and in small villages throughout the country. Since the union of the two Yemens, however, many people have left the rural areas in search of jobs in the cities.

FAST FACTS

✔ **Official name:** Republic of Yemen

✔ **Capital:** Sana'a

✔ **Location:** Middle East bordering the Arabian Sea, Gulf of Aden, and Red Sea, between Oman and Saudi Arabia

✔ **Area:** 203,850 square miles (527,970 square kilometers)

✔ **Population:** 19,349,881 (July 2003 est.)

✔ **Age distribution:**
0–14 years: 47%
15–64 years: 50%
over 65 years: 3%

✔ **Life expectancy:**
Males: 59 years
Females: 63 years

✔ **Ethnic groups:** Arab, Afro-Arab, South Asian, and European

✔ **Religions:** Muslim, including the Sunni and Shi'a sects, small numbers of Jews, Christians, and Hindus

✔ **Languages:** Arabic

✔ **Currency:**
Yemeni rial (YER)
US$1 = 177 YER

✔ **Average annual income:** US$450

✔ **Major exports:** Crude oil, coffee, dried and salted fish

Source: CIA, *The World Factbook 2002;* BBC News Country Profiles.

During the Persian Gulf War (1991), Saudi Arabia expelled hundreds of thousands of Yemeni workers because of Yemen's support of Iraq. This sudden influx created even more pressure on the economy, and unemployment rates soared.

Religious status, occupations, and family connections determine the social status of most Yemenis. Most of the people belong to one of two branches of Islam: Sunni or Shi'a. At the top of the social ladder are the Zaydis, a Shi'a sect based in northwestern Yemen. They are the second largest Shi'a sect and are descendants of Mohammed. Zaydis are respected for their important government positions, wealth, education, and religious knowledge. For many years, this group received special privileges. They held high legal positions and had access to advanced education. Many own large pieces of farmland. Today, the wealthy Zaydis still hold important positions in Yemeni society.

The Qadis are another elite group. They are Islamic legal scholars, and most are descended from the rulers who led Yemen before the spread of Islam. Their social status is inherited. The Qadis are generally well educated and are respected for their wisdom.

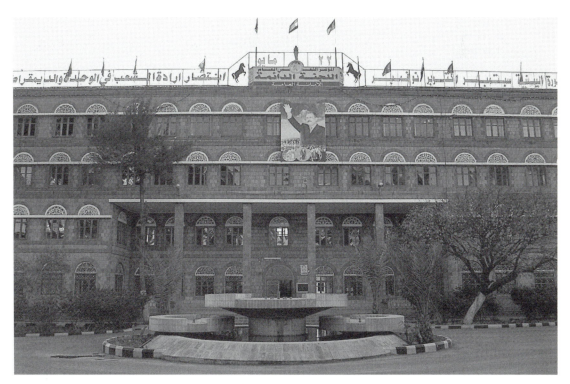

Headquarters of the General People's Congress, the ruling party of Yemen since 1990. The government of Yemen has committed itself to socioeconomic development and making significant progress toward democracy.

Below these two groups on the social ladder are the tribal people of Qahtani ancestry. The Qahtani are farmers who are headed by a sheikh. The sheikh oversees the village and has the power to settle disputes within the community.

Artisans and merchants are ranked by their occupations. Their ancestry is not known, so they are considered below the Qahtani in the social order. Skilled crafts workers such as blacksmiths and goldsmiths are more respected than less skilled workers such as barbers or butchers, who are sometimes called *muzayyin.* In recent years, attitudes have been changing about these lower groups. Services performed by the *muzayyin* have become more respected. As education for all social classes increases, literacy is becoming more widespread.

Land and Resources

Geography

Yemen is a country of mountains, plains, and deserts. It has no rivers, but many *wadis,* or dry riverbeds, cut through the landscape. The wadis fill with water during the rainy season. Yemen can be divided into four regions: the coastal plain or Tihama in northern Yemen, the mountains of the Western and Central Highlands, the eastern region and desert, and the islands.

The Tihama is a flat coastal plain that ranges in width from 15 to 40 miles (24 to 64 kilometers). It runs parallel to the Red Sea and extends from the southern tip of Yemen northward into Saudi Arabia. Some parts of this sandy plain are made fertile by irrigation. It is very hot and humid and few people live there.

The plains end at a series of rocky cliffs that meet the mountains of the Western Highlands. These mountains are made of lava and form peaks that reach more than 10,000 feet (3,048 meters). The highest mountain in Yemen—and the Arabian Peninsula—is Jabal al-Nabi Shuayb, which towers more than 12,000 feet (3,660 meters) high. Moving eastward, the mountains level off and become the fertile, high plateau of the Central Highlands. This region is home to Yemen's urban centers, productive farmland, and the capital city of Sana'a.

The eastern region of Yemen is a sandy coastal plain that borders the Gulf of Aden and the Arabian Desert in the north. Beyond the inland hills of al-Mashriq is the Rub al-Khali, or Empty Quarter, a sandy desert that extends into Saudi Arabia. The desert is the home of Bedouin herders who herd their livestock across the desert from one watering hole to another and from one grazing land to the next.

Narrow wadis that irrigate the land for farming cut through this area. Wadi Hadhramawt, the largest wadi, stretches across the entire region from east to west before turning south and emptying into the Arabian Sea. This wadi is known for the date and frankincense trees that grow near it.

Yemen has about 112 islands. Socotra—at 1,400 square miles (3,600 square kilometers), the largest island in Yemen—is located off the tip of Somalia in the Arabian Sea. Yemen also controls the islands of Kamaran and Perim and the Hanish Islands, which include four main islands. Each island has its own distinct climate and geography.

Major Cities

Yemen is still a predominantly rural country. It has many small villages, but only a few cities. The main cities are Sana'a and Aden. Today, only about a quarter of the population lives in the urban areas. Job opportunities have slowly increased the migration of people from villages to the cities.

This small town lies just west of Sana'a, one of the most ancient cities in the Arab world. The city, now a growing urban environment, is the home of the Great Mosque of Sana'a. The surrounding towns and landscapes are rich with historic architecture and archaeological significance.

Sana'a

As well as being the oldest city in Yemen, Sana'a is the largest and most important city. Its name means "fortified place," referring to a time when the rulers of ancient Yemen used the city as a fortress. Sana'a lies about 140 miles (225 kilometers) east of the Red Sea and about halfway between the Gulf of Aden and the northern border. The capital city has experienced a population explosion since the early 1970s, growing from 55,000 people to 1.5 million. Today, the city's main inhabitants are Muslim Arabs.

Visitors to Sana'a often stop to visit the Rock Palace, the summer residence built by the monarch Imam Yahya in the 1930s. It was recently renovated and reopened to the public.

Sana'a is famous for its *medina,* or old walled city, that was established in the first century C.E. Many of the buildings within the walled city are over 800 years old. As the city grew, many wealthy residents moved to the outskirts of Sana'a, leaving the buildings in the medina to deteriorate. In recent years, the United Nations has funded the restoration and preservation of the medina.

In the southeastern section of the medina is the Suq al-Milh, or central market. There, shoppers can find anything from pottery, clothes, and carpets to silver and copper goods. Farmers sell vegetables and spices.

Aden

Aden was built in the crater of an extinct volcano on the southern coast of Yemen. During ancient times, Aden was an important commercial center. Today, it serves as Yemen's chief seaport and is still considered the commercial capital of the country. Modern roads connect Aden to other cities and villages throughout the country, and foreign ships stop at the port to load fish products, coffee, cotton, and salt. In addition to being a manufacturing center for cooking oil and textiles, Aden has a large oil refinery.

Climate

Yemen's climate varies considerably according to elevation and location. The Western and Central Highlands are drier and cooler than the rest of the country. During the winter season, which runs from December to February, temperatures can drop below freezing. Rainfall is scarce along the Red Sea and the southern coast. This region is hot and humid all year long. Temperatures often reach 104° F (40° C) during the summer months. The desert and eastern regions are extremely hot. Temperatures soar to 122° F (50° C) during the day but drop dramatically when the sun sets.

DUST STORMS

The *shammal* is a great dust storm that blows from the northwest across the Red Sea to the coastal areas of Yemen. During the *shammal,* extremely high winds pick up particles of clay and sand that scrape away the surface of rocks and other objects in their path. The *shammal* can even remove paint from an automobile. Dust storms also destroy crops and erode the soil. At times, the wind can become so full of sand that it blocks the sun. Airports often have to close during July and August when the *shammal* arrives.

Natural Resources

Oil and natural gas generate a large portion of Yemen's income. Oil was discovered near Shabwah in central Yemen in 1983 and near Ma'rib in west-central Yemen in 1984. By 1986, Yemen had opened oil wells and built pipelines to transport oil to the Red Sea coast.

Yemen mines large quantities of salt and marble. Because of the country's need for cement and stone to build homes and buildings, there is a great demand for these resources.

Some of the most fertile land in the Arabian Peninsula is found in Yemen. More than half of the population farms for a living. The farms produce enough food for the local communities. They also raise cattle, goats, and sheep. Most recently, chicken farms have begun to be established as the demand for eggs increases. The most common crops are wheat, barley, millet, and corn. Fruits such as mangoes, bananas, apricots, and grapes are grown in the Central Highlands.

For years, coffee has been the most important export in Yemen. The Central highlands offer the best environment for growing coffee.

Both the Red Sea and the Arabian Sea are rich with shrimp, lobster, and tuna. In the past, Yemeni fishermen did not have the money or equipment to develop this resource. With technical and financial support from the former Soviet Union, however, the fishing industry is playing an increased role in Yemen's economy, supported by new processing plants that facilitate the export of seafood.

Plants and Animals

The Western Highlands receive enough rain to support many flowering bushes, including acacias and ficus. Date, mango, and papaya trees are also found there, and cotton is a major crop.

Almond, walnut, peach, and apricot trees grow in the Central Highlands. A variety of grapevines and spice plants also grow in this region. The Central Highlands are home to eucalyptus, sycamore, fig, and carob trees. Coffee is grown in the mountain regions.

Today, because of population growth and agriculture, less than 6 percent of the country has any forests. Farmers cleared the land to plant crops and used the wood for fuel and building materials.

As recently as a century ago, panthers, ostrich, antelopes, and rhinoceros were found in Yemen. Hunting has contributed to a decline in many species, as has the continued growth of the population, which intrudes on the animals' habitats. Today, the largest mammal still found in the wild is the gelada baboon, which lives in the mountains and highlands of northwest Yemen. Smaller animals, such as foxes, wolves, and hyenas, still live in the wild.

Many species of birds can be seen in Yemen. Only thirteen species are native to the country, but nearly 300 species of migratory birds stop in Yemen on their way to Europe and central Asia.

The desert is home to the desert viper (a type of snake), scorpions, and locusts. Locusts travel in hordes searching for food. Each year they descend on farms and can destroy entire crops within minutes.

The falcon, a large bird of prey, is used only for sport hunting in Yemen.

History

Ancient Days

Archaeologists have found flint tools and stone dwellings to substantiate their claim that Yemen has been inhabited since 5000 B.C.E. Around 2000 B.C.E., people believed to be the descendants of Noah settled in northwest Yemen.

By 1000 B.C.E., Yemen was the site of several prosperous kingdoms. Saba (known as Sheba in the Old Testament of the Bible) and Minaean in the Central Highlands and Hadhramawt in eastern Yemen were the three most famous and largest empires. According to archaeologists, these kingdoms seem to have lived in peace. They shared a common faith based on polytheism, the worship of many gods.

Saba, which endured for fourteen centuries, was the largest and wealthiest of the kingdoms and probably the most powerful. It prospered from trade and agriculture. Known for their building skills, the Sabeans built an intricate irrigation system that enabled farmers to grow crops in areas with little or no water. This system included dams that channeled occasional rainwater into canals. The largest dam was the Marib dam, built around 500 B.C.E. near Marib, the capital of Saba.

The trade routes started in southern and western Arabia and crossed into Mesopotamia and Babylonia (present-day Iraq), Egypt, Palestine (modern Israel), and Syria. Large caravans of camels carried

THE MARIB DAM

The Marib Dam, built southwest of Marib in the Balaq Mountains, is one of the most famous ancient Yemeni ruins. The dam was built of huge pieces of stone and covered with volcanic stones. Its irrigation network, linked to drains on both sides of the dam, is considered the most sophisticated engineering work of ancient times. More than 27 square miles (70 square kilometers) of land in the Marib Valley were cultivated with the help of the dam's irrigation network.

The dam collapsed and was renovated several times. The last work done on the dam was in the sixth century B.C.E. The wall at the tip of the dam still exists today.

IMPORTANT EVENTS IN YEMEN'S HISTORY

2000 B.C.E. Semitic people settle in northwest Yemen.

1000 B.C.E. Trade routes develop between Yemeni kingdoms and northern Arabia.

900s B.C.E. The Queen of Sheba rules southern Arabia (known today as Yemen).

525 C.E. Ethiopia invades Yemen.

575 Persia conquers Yemeni kingdoms.

628 People in Yemen convert to Islam.

897 Zaydi dynasty is established in the north.

1173 Ayyubid rulers from Egypt conquer Yemen.

1548 The Ottoman Empire takes over Yemen.

1839 Britain gains control of Aden.

1869 The Suez Canal opens and serves as a major port for refueling.

1904 The Ottomans and Britain sign a treaty that establishes a border between north and south Yemen.

1911 The Ottomans and the Zaydis sign the Treaty of Da'an that gives the Zaydis power in the north.

1918 The Ottomans withdraw from northern Yemen following their defeat in World War I. The international community recognizes North Yemen as an independent state ruled by Yahya ibn Muhammad.

1934 Saudi Arabia and North Yemen engage in a war.

1948 Liberal reformers assassinate Imam Yahya. Imam Ahmad, Yahya's son, takes over in the north.

1959 Britain forms the Federation of the Arab Emirates of the South, which later becomes the Federation of South Arabia.

1962 North Yemen becomes known as the Yemen Arab Republic (YAR).

1963 A nationalist group in South Yemen forms the National Liberation Front (NLF). War breaks out near Aden between the NLF and Britain.

1967 The NLF forces Britain to withdraw from South Yemen. The NLF declares the People's Republic of South Yemen an independent country under the leadership of Qahtan al-Shabi.

1970 The People's Republic of South Yemen becomes known as the People's Democratic Republic of Yemen (PDRY).

1970 Civil war in the north comes to an end. Saudi Arabia forms ties with the YAR.

1972 Border disputes between north (YAR) and south (PDRY) Yemen erupt into hostile conflicts.

1978 Colonel Ali Abdullah Saleh becomes president of YAR.

1989 Oil is discovered in north Yemen. Yemeni leaders agree on a timetable to merge the south and north into one country.

1990 Yemenis approve a new constitution, and the two countries are unified. The new country is called the Republic of Yemen. Saleh becomes president of Yemen, and Ali Salim al-Baid from the south becomes vice president.

1991 Yemen opposes the Gulf War in Iraq, which is led by the United States.

1993 Vice President Ali Salim al-Baid moves to Aden, alleging that the northerners are attacking the southerners.

1994 Saleh dismisses al-Baid and other southern government officials following political disagreements and fighting. Northern armies take control of Aden.

2000 Terrorists associated with Al Qaeda attack the U.S.S. *Cole,* a U.S. naval vessel in Aden.

2001 Saleh visits U.S. president George W. Bush and offers support in the fight against terrorism.

2002 Terrorists set off an explosion off the Yemeni coast that damages the supertanker *Limburg.*

frankincense and myrrh, strong-smelling resins from trees that grew in eastern Yemen. Myrrh was an important ingredient in cosmetics, perfumes, and medicines. Frankincense was incense that was burned in religious ceremonies. Traders also sold spices and textiles from India, gold and ivory from Africa, and fine silks from China. The goods from other countries were shipped to the port of Aden and transported by camels along the Incense Road into other countries. So many valuable riches came from southern Arabia that the northern merchants began calling it Arabia Felix, which means "happy Arabia" in Latin.

Decline of the Kingdoms

In the first century C.E., a Mediterranean seaman named Hippalus discovered a direct sea route between Egypt and India. The center of trade shifted west to the coast of the Red Sea. This new trade route led to the rise of Himyar, a kingdom in the highlands. By 50 C.E., the Himyarites ruled southern Arabia, including Yemen, and took control of the shipping routes.

The caravan trails were no longer useful, and the loss of trade to India was a major force in the decline of Saba. The economic decline in the kingdoms made it impossible for them to maintain their wealth and

THE QUEEN OF SHEBA

The kingdom of Saba—known as *Sheba* in Hebrew—is best known for its queen. The legendary Sabean queen Bilqis, known as the Queen of Sheba, is written about in the Old Testament and the Qur'an. The Queen of Sheba was the ruler over the most powerful kingdom in southern Arabia. She had great influence over the southern part of the Incense Road, while King Solomon controlled the northern end of the route. The two powerful rulers met in ancient Palestine and, by some accounts, had a child together.

In 1998, Canadian archaeologists working in Marib began excavating the 3,000-year-old Temple of the Moon God, a sacred site that drew pilgrims from throughout Arabia. The six columns seen in the photo provide entrance to the Throne of Bilqis. Many

artifacts from ancient Saba have been uncovered among the ruins, among them documents related to the Queen of Sheba's reign and 2,000-year-old frankincense.

prestige. Consequently, in 525 C.E., when the Great Dam at Marib ruptured, Saba did not have the money to repair it. The economy continued to plummet because of this loss of irrigation for farming.

Another factor in the decline of the kingdoms was the spread of the Roman Empire. The Romans had conquered the area from northern Europe into North Africa. In 323 C.E., Christianity was proclaimed as the official religion. Because Christianity did not allow the use of incense for religious rituals, there was no demand for frankincense and myrrh.

The ruling Himyarites allowed missionaries of other faiths to enter Yemen. Christian and Jewish missionaries were successful in converting the people of southern Arabia. In the early sixth century, the Sabean king ordered all Christians to convert to Judaism. More than 20,000 Christians refused and were executed. In response, the Christian king of Ethiopia took control of Yemen in 525. After his death, forty-five years later, the Himyarites asked Persia to get rid of the Ethiopians. So, in 575, the Yemeni kingdoms came under Persian rule.

The Spread of Islam

In the early part of the seventh century a new religion sprang up across the Arabian Peninsula. Islam, which was founded by the Arab prophet Mohammad, quickly spread throughout Yemen. Many Yemeni sheikhs converted to Islam and introduced this new religion to their people. By the 630s, the first mosque was built in Sana'a.

In 661 the Umayyad Dynasty took over leadership of Yemen and moved its capital from Mecca to Damascus. Yemen became a province of the Umayyad Empire. In 750 the Abbasid clan overthrew the Umayyads and established the capital in Baghdad (in modern-day Iraq). This allowed several small, independent kingdoms to develop in southern Arabia.

The most significant event in the history of Yemen after the introduction of Islam was the formation of the Zaydi (an Islamic Shi'a sect) Dynasty in northern Yemen in 897. A descendant of Mohammad, al-Rassi, became the first *imam* (spiritual leader) of the Zaydi Dynasty when he was asked to mediate a war between two rival clans in northwestern Yemen. The Zaydis' beliefs were similar to those of Sunni Muslims. Rassi's teachings centered on an active role for the imam and emphasized the study of war, which enabled the Zaydis to survive centuries of attacks.

In 1173 the Ayyubid rulers of Egypt conquered Yemen. It was made a self-governing state within the Ayyubid Empire. Political power was left to a local official, Nur al-Din Umar ibn al-Rasul, who proclaimed Yemen an independent nation. The Rasulid family ruled Yemen from 1228 to 1454.

Foreign Invasions

At the beginning of the fifteenth century, coffee was becoming a popular beverage. Yemen and the Red Sea became an area of conflict between the Egyptians and the Ottomans, who were trying to gain control over the trade of Indian spices and the emerging coffee industry. This conflict continued during most of the sixteenth and seventeenth centuries.

In the early 1500s, the Europeans, including Portuguese merchants, turned their attention to the lucrative trade route between Egypt and India. They wanted to control the Red Sea and Arabian coastal ports. In 1507 the Portuguese annexed the island of Socotra in the Indian Ocean, just outside the Gulf of Aden. In 1513, a Portuguese conqueror, Alfonso de Albuquerque, tried unsuccessfully to dominate the port of Aden. To protect its interests, Egypt captured Tihama, the flat coastal area that extends from the southern tip of Yemen northward into Saudi Arabia and the highlands around today's capital city of Sana'a. However, the Egyptians' attack on Aden failed.

By 1517 the Ottoman Empire, with its capital in Istanbul (in present-day Turkey), had become the greatest military power in the Mediterranean. It conquered Egypt in that same year. In 1548 the Ottomans arrived in Yemen and took control of the country.

The Ottoman rule lasted for more than a century. During that time trade with Europe grew. There was also a growing global interest in the coffee industry. The port of Mocha in Yemen became a central point in the coffee trade.

Although the cities were prosperous, many Yemenis resented the occupation of the Ottomans in Yemen. In 1590, Qasim the Great, a descendant of the Zaydi imams, began to exploit that resentment against the Ottomans. Shi'a and Sunni Muslims supported Qasim in his quest to take over the region. By 1608, Qasim was elected imam and had gained enough support from the Muslim citizens to force the Ottomans into a ten-year truce. The Ottomans were finally expelled from Yemen in 1636 when Qasim's son Muayyad Muhammad came into power.

Zaydi rule lasted more than 200 years. The Zaydi region extended east to Hadhramawt and north to the coastal region of Asir in present-day Saudi Arabia. Centralized control of Yemen fell apart when some groups began to claim their independence. In 1728 the Sultan of Lahej in the south blocked Zaydi access to the port of Aden.

At the same time the British were looking for a coaling station on the route to India. The unrest in South Yemen gave them the chance to increase their influence in the area. In 1799, they seized the island of Perim, which lies near the Bab al-Mandab strait that separates the Gulf of Aden and the Red Sea. In 1839 Britain occupied the port city of Aden.

In 1849 the Ottomans returned to Yemen and occupied the Tihama region in order to keep the British from taking over control of the Red Sea. In 1869 the Suez Canal was opened, connecting the Mediterranean Sea to the Gulf of Suez and then to the Red Sea. This prompted the Ottomans to expand their territory into the highlands to keep the British from taking control of the entire Red Sea.

By 1882 the Ottomans had seized control of most of southwestern Yemen, including the Zaydi capital of Sadah. The British were concerned about the Ottoman expansion. To protect Aden from a takeover, they extended their control to the tribal states around Aden. The British signed treaties with Yemeni tribal leaders, giving them

Many of the earliest settled parts of Yemen still stand today. These traditional or "loam" houses are built around the mosque of Sadah.

military protection if they would not give away any of their land without British approval. The area became known as the Aden Protectorate.

In 1904 the Ottomans and the British drew the border between their two territories. This created North and South Yemen, a boundary that lasted until 1990.

North Yemen

The people living in North Yemen opposed the occupation of the Ottomans. Throughout the early 1900s, the Zaydis and other northern Tihama tribes organized many resistance movements under the leadership of Sayyid Mohammed al-Idrisi. In 1911 the Ottomans and the Zaydis signed the Treaty of Da'an, which gave the Zaydis power over the highlands.

The Treaty of Lausanne, signed in 1924, marked an end to World War I and officially ended the reign of the Ottomans in Yemen. North Yemen was granted its independence under Zaydi leader Yahya ibn Muhammad. The imam wanted to claim all of "historic Yemen" as his own, including the protectorates and Aden as well as the Saudi province of Asir and the areas around the Najran oasis. In 1925 he defeated Idrisi forces in the Tihama, who by that time were *allied* with Saudi Arabia.

Yahya's advances north alarmed the Saudis and resulted in the Saudi-Yemeni War of 1934. The conflict ended with the signing of the Taif Treaty, which established a short, northwestern boundary between the two countries. Asir and Najran were temporarily under Saudi rule.

Fear of losing his power caused Imam Yahya to rule North Yemen by isolating it from outside influences. He soon realized that he needed foreign technology, which required Yemenis to get training and education. In the 1930s he allowed the first Yemenis to go abroad to study. Exposed to outside ideas and leadership, some Yemenis began to question Yahya's policies.

In 1948 the dissent of some Yemenis led to the assassination of Imam Yahya. Yahya's son Imam Ahmad assumed power and established his own government, which was much like his father's. By the end of his reign in 1962, North Yemen still had poor roads, no schools, and few factories.

Yemen Arab Republic

After the death of Imam Ahmad in 1962, his son Mohammed al-Badr came to power. One week into his reign, a group led by Colonel

Abdullah Sallal overthrew al-Badr. The new regime with Sallal as president founded the Yemen Arab Republic (YAR). The YAR soon became a member of the United Nations.

Imam al-Badr fled to the mountains and formed a resistance group to regain his power. A civil war began in 1962 with the imam's royalist group supported by Saudi Arabia and Britain while Egypt and the Soviet Union backed the Republicans (YAR). There were many casualties on both sides. By 1967, the two sides had reached a stalemate. There was internal fighting within the Republican army. President Sallal believed the only way to win the war was to establish a relationship with Saudi Arabia. Many Republicans in his troops did not agree. As a result, these anti-Saudi Republicans replaced Sallal with President al-Iryani. The war ended in 1970 when Imam al-Badr was exiled.

South Yemen

In the 1830s, the British divided South Yemen into three parts: the Aden colony and the western and eastern protectorates. (A *protectorate* is a country that depends upon a foreign government for security.) Britain ruled the protectorates through local leaders and intervened only when necessary. Although there was some unrest in the Aden colony, the port of Aden grew and prospered, becoming a hub of trading activity.

Residents of Aden wanted independence for the colony, so Britain promised to grant independence to the federation at a later date. A left-wing *nationalist* group formed the National Liberation Front (NLF) in 1963 and staged an uprising. The NLF forced the collapse of the federation in 1967 and the British withdrew from South Yemen.

The new country was under the leadership of Qahtan al-Shabi. Due to the closing of the Suez Canal in 1967, South Yemen lost British trade and investment and was faced with economic difficulties. It allied itself with the Soviet Union and other communist countries for financial support. The country's political policies began to closely resemble those of other Communist nations. In 1969 al-Shabi was removed from power in favor of Salim Rubay Ali, who was strongly pro-communist. He brought most of the country's economy under government control, changing the name of the country to the People's Democratic Republic of Yemen (PDRY) in 1970.

Unification

By the early 1970s, the economies of both the YAR and the PDRY were in shambles because of many years of conflict. Both countries relied heavily on foreign aid. The YAR received money from Saudi Arabia and Europe, while the Soviet Union aided the PDRY. The hostile relationship between the Soviets and the Saudis put the two Yemens at odds. This resulted in a series of wars along their borders.

During this time, the two major powers in the world, the United States and the Soviet Union, were both leading nuclear powers competing for global influence. The United States sought to keep the Soviet Union from controlling other countries and gaining more power by spreading communism. Saudi Arabia, which held the same views as the United States, opposed the Soviet support of south Yemen.

In 1972, the prime ministers of the Soviet Union and Saudi Arabia agreed on a time line for a merger of the two Yemens. However, this merger never took place because the leaders of both countries were unable to sway the voting members of their governments to accept *unification*.

In 1978, after the leadership of the YAR had changed hands many times, Colonel Ali Abdullah Saleh became president. The YAR steadily improved its economy and relations with foreign countries. However, the PDRY had many internal political conflicts. The economic decline

Despite ongoing political problems, a united Yemen has improved the country's economy and national morale.

of the Soviet Union forced the Soviets to close their naval base at Aden and reduce financial aid to the PDRY.

In 1989 oil and natural gas were found in both countries at roughly the same time and in the same geographic region. It was in the best interest of both countries to unite and share these resources. Another factor that led to this merger was Soviet president Mikhail Gorbachev's decision to abandon financial support of South Yemen. In 1990 the two Yemens finally merged. The new country was renamed the Republic of Yemen. Ali Abdullah Saleh, a member of the General People's Congress (GPC), became president, and Ali Salim al-Baid from the Yemeni Socialist Party (YSP) in the south became vice president. Sana'a, the former capital of North Yemen, became the political capital of the new country, while Aden became the economic center.

Under the leadership of Saleh and with financial aid from foreign countries such as Iraq, Saudi Arabia, and Kuwait, Yemen's economy began to expand. In 1990 the invasion of Kuwait by Iraqi forces led to the Persian Gulf War between Iraq and United Nations forces in Saudi Arabia. Yemen's position on the Persian Gulf jeopardized the aid it was receiving from all the parties involved in the war. Yemen was against the Gulf War and it also criticized the presence of foreign troops in Saudi Arabia. In retaliation, Saudi Arabia evicted more than 600,000 Yemenis working there. These workers, returning home to Yemen, created a large unemployment problem.

Yemen Today

In 1994, the GPC and the YSP had a disagreement over the sharing of power. A civil war broke out between the supporters of the president and those of the vice president. Within a few months, those supporting the president won the war. President Saleh dismissed Vice President al-Baid and other members of the government who had supported al-Baid.

Ali Abdullah Saleh was reelected president in 1999. This was Yemen's first presidential election. However, the opposition party was not allowed to have a candidate in the election.

In October 2000, a United States naval vessel docked in the port of Aden was bombed by the group Al Qaeda. The United States government believes that Al Qaeda is an international terrorist network (this Arabic word means "the base") led by Osama bin Laden. This terrorist group is dedicated to opposing non-Islamic governments with force and violence. The link between some Yemenis and Osama bin Laden, the suspected leader of Al Qaeda, goes back at least to 1989, when over 40,000 Yemeni volunteers fought alongside bin Laden in the struggle against the Soviet occupation in Afghanistan. The attack on the U.S.S. *Cole* had widespread support in Yemen. Since that time, the United States Navy has heightened its patrol of the Yemen coast in hopes of preventing Al Qaeda fighters from finding refuge in Yemen.

Today, Yemen is trying to rid itself of its reputation as a safe haven for Muslim militants. In 2001 President Saleh met with U.S. president George Bush to offer support in the fight against terrorism. Despite urging from the United States, President Saleh has chosen to fight this war with negotiation rather than military force. He is not fully convinced that there is enough evidence linking Osama bin Laden to terrorist attacks on the World Trade Center in New York City in 2001. In February 2002, Yemen expelled more than 100 foreign Islamic scholars as part of a crackdown on suspected Al Qaeda members.

Economy

Throughout history, agriculture and fishing have been important to Yemen's economy. Before and after unification, Yemen depended on the financial aid of foreign countries from the United States, Europe, and the former Soviet Union. Since the discovery of oil in the 1980s, oil production has significantly contributed to the economy.

Yemen's support of Saddam Hussein during the Gulf War dramatically increased unemployment rates in the country. The expulsion of Yemeni citizens from Saudi Arabia in 1990 and 1991 sent thousands of workers back to their homeland. In addition, thousands of refugees fleeing hunger and war in Somalia entered Yemen in 1992, hoping to find jobs that never materialized.

Business and Industry

Although the manufacturing of bricks, tiles, and other building materials is growing, there are still few factories in Yemen. Oil refining is currently the most important industry. Yemen has expanded its industry by building factories that manufacture processed food, aluminum, cigarettes, and soft drinks.

Government and trade services generate half of Yemen's national output. To attract more tourism, the government has plans to expand

and modernize hotels, convention centers, and restaurants. But tourism has been hindered by the threat of kidnapping. Some foreigners have been kidnapped by tribes and held hostage for ransom or as bargaining chips for various factions to make gains with the government.

The poor transportation system in Yemen has slowed the export of goods. Until recently, camels and donkeys were still being used as the main mode of transportation. The government has made an increased effort to connect agricultural regions and industrial cities with roads, but progress is slow. Yemen exports goods such as crude oil, coffee, salt, dates, and cotton using its docks and airports. The United States is Yemen's largest trading partner.

Media and Communications

The Ministry of Information controls all public radio and television broadcasting and the printing of newspapers. Newspapers are often prosecuted when they publish articles critical of the government. Yemen publishes hundreds of newspapers. The *Yemen Times* is an English-language paper that is very outspoken against government policies. As of 2001, 17,000 people in Yemen used the Internet.

Yemeni men read the news of the day. Freedom of the press in Yemen has greatly deteriorated since the war in 1994. Newspapers featuring articles that are critical of state policies risk closure by the government. Yemeni journalists may face severe punishment and imprisonment if they speak out or publish articles against their leaders.

Even with poor reception due to the mountains, some families have televisions. In many villages, neighbors gather in the few homes that have a television. Two networks broadcast programs from Sana'a and Aden between the hours of 4:00 P.M. and midnight when electricity is available. As satellite dishes become more popular, news coverage and television shows from other countries are reaching Yemeni homes.

Religion and Beliefs

Islam

The state religion of Yemen is Islam. Most Yemenis are Muslims. Muslims follow the teachings of the Prophet Mohammad, who established Islam in the seventh century. They believe in one God— Allah—who revealed the Qur'an, the Muslim holy book (commonly known in the West as the Koran) to Mohammad, the last in a series of prophets that includes Abraham and Jesus. (To learn more about Islam, see pages ix–xii in the introduction to this volume.)

About half of Yemen's population are Sunni Muslims living in southern Yemen. A third to a half of the Yemeni Muslims are Zaydis, a Shi'a subgroup that once ruled the country and still influences the government.

The practice of Islam is of chief importance in the life of most Yemenis.

The Shi'a believe that Muslim leadership should be descended from Ali, Mohammed's cousin. The Sunnis believe that elected members of the community can become leaders. Although some of their laws differ, both sects agree on most of the major matters of faith and worship.

Other Religions

The Jewish population in Yemen is small; however, it represents the largest non-Muslim group in the country. The population declined rapidly after 1948, when Israel became a nation. Most Yemeni Jews have moved to Israel.

In addition to Jews, small communities of Christians and Hindus live in southern Yemen.

Everyday Life

Everyday life is varies among the Yemeni farmers, herders, crafts workers, and professionals. In rural areas, daily living is very strenuous, while the cities foster contemporary lifestyles. However, all groups share a similar set of values. Allegiance to the family is a higher priority than allegiance to society.

An increasing number of Yemeni women are integrated with men in the workforce outside the home. However, women are still separated from men for many social activities, and most Yemeni women do not eat in public restaurants. In general, women in the south, particularly in Aden, are better educated and have had somewhat greater employment opportunities than women in northern Yemen. However, since the 1994 war of secession, the number of working women in the south appears to have declined, due not only to the slowing economy but also to increasing cultural pressure from the north. Today, female employees account for only 19 percent of the paid labor force.

Family Life

Families are extremely important to the Yemenis. It is not unusual to find many relatives living in the same house. The head of the household is the father, and the mother raises the children, cooks, and cleans. The men are in charge of any task, such as going to the market, that requires contact with the public.

Children are considered gifts from God. Large families are highly valued in rural areas where there is much work to be done. On average,

Yemeni women have six children. The older children look after younger siblings and work in the fields to harvest the crops. Since it is becoming harder to make a living from the land, some women are choosing to have fewer children so that the family can afford to educate them to get better jobs.

Since Yemen is an Islamic country, the families arrange most marriages. Men have little opportunity to meet or speak with women, so they take the advice of their mothers and sisters about whom to marry.

Dress

The clothing of a Yemeni man identifies where he comes from, his tribe, and his position in society. Traditional tribal attire for men is a *futa* (FOO-ta), which is a wraparound skirt, a turban, and a dagger. The dagger is kept in a sheath (knife case) and is worn in the center of the body. It is kept in place by a leather or cloth belt. The way a man wraps his turban around his head tells what tribe he belongs to. Trends in clothing are changing, however. In the cities, more men are wearing suits or combining traditional clothing with modern attire, while tribal attire is becoming popular among nontribesmen.

Yemeni men mix the old with the new in their style of dress. Although Yemen is a rapidly modernizing country, with some evidence of Western influence in the cities of Sana'a and Aden, most of the country is still rooted in traditional Islamic culture.

Most women in Yemen wear pants or tights under their dresses. They are required to cover all parts of their bodies whenever they leave their homes. Their heads are covered with veils and scarves. Rural women may wear more than one scarf to cover their heads. In western Yemen, many women wear hats instead of veils. In the urban areas, women wear a veil over their face and quite often wear a *sharshaf,* a loosely fitted black garment that covers their bodies.

> Although Yemeni women have access to European cosmetics, they still paint their skin with traditional designs for special occasions. For religious festivals, women use a dye called *khidah* to create floral designs on their hands and feet.

Education

Less than half of the people who are 15 years old and older can read and write, in part because, for much of Yemen's history, only the wealthy could afford an education. According to government statistics for 2000, about 68 percent of Yemeni women were illiterate compared with about 28 percent of men. This percentage was higher among women because until recently they were not encouraged to get an education.

The current constitution states that all citizens have a right to an education. There are public schools in the cities and larger towns. In rural areas, there are Muslim religious schools. Yemen's first university, the University of Sana'a, was founded in 1970. Aden is also home to a university.

In recent years, more Yemeni women have begun to attend universities and training programs. The literacy rate in the cities is rising quickly among girls, while there is only 1 girl for every 10 boys that attend school in the rural areas.

Recreation and Leisure

The Yemeni culture allows plenty of time for socializing. Men and women spend time visiting and exchanging gossip throughout the day as they attend the mosque or the market. Some offices will close for afternoon gatherings. However, these are not coed activities. Bathhouses are common for people who can afford them. On separate days, men and women visit the bathhouses, exercise, and visit with friends.

Since families are so important, many leisure activities include the entire family. Soccer is a favorite pastime among children. Boys are often seen kicking a ball around the village or city. There are very few professional athletes in Yemen. The country has competed in three Olympic Games, but Yemeni athletes have never won a medal.

After their household chores are finished, Yemeni children play with their friends. The children often play games such as dominoes or backgammon. Cards and marbles are also popular with the boys. Girls like to play with dolls or make up their own games. They may even have poetry contests, creating and reciting their own poems.

Food

The noon meal is considered the most important of the day. If guests are invited, the men will eat first and then the women join them. Otherwise the family will eat together. The women in the family are responsible for preparing the food.

Islam is a major influence on food and drink, since Muslims do not eat pork or drink alcohol. The Yemeni diet is quite simple, making use of locally grown grains, fruits, and vegetables. Rice, bread, vegetables, lamb, and fish are the primary foods. Bread is eaten at every meal. Every day the Yemeni women bake enough bread for the day. The national dish is a spicy stew called *saltah*. It is a meat or chicken broth with vegetables that is eaten with a special flatbread. Another well-known dish is *ful*, which is a mixture of beans, uncooked vegetables, and oil.

Yemenis share their food generously. It is offensive to the host if a guest refuses food when offered. While eating at home, the Yemenis sit on the floor, and the food is served in pots and arranged on a silk cloth. No utensils are used. Food is taken from the pot by scooping with bread. The right hand is always used for eating, since the left hand is considered unclean in Islamic tradition.

SALATAT TAMATIM WA KUZBARA

(Tomato and Coriander Salad)

Coriander has been used in cooking since ancient times. The Chinese believed that coriander could lead to immortality, while Egyptians often left coriander seeds in their tombs, apparently as a food offering to the gods. (In North America, the leaves of the herb are generally known as cilantro.)

5 medium tomatoes, diced
1/8 cup fresh coriander leaves (cilantro), chopped

1/8 teaspoon cayenne
3 tablespoons lemon juice
2 tablespoons olive oil
Salt and pepper to taste

Combine the tomatoes and coriander leaves in a salad bowl. In a separate bowl, thoroughly mix the remaining ingredients. Pour over the tomatoes and toss just before serving.

Adapted from *From the Lands of Figs and Olives* by Habeeb Salloum.

Although coffee from the port of Mocha is world-famous, it is not as widely drunk as tea because it is too expensive.

Holidays and Festivals

Ramadan, the month during which Muslims fast from sunrise to sunset, is one of the most significant religious observances in the Islamic world. The self-discipline required for the fast shows one's devotion to Allah, while experiencing hunger and thirst encourages empathy for those who are poor and hungry all year long.

Before sunrise each morning of Ramadan, a drummer wanders the streets to waken the neighborhood. Muslims eat a small meal and then fast until sunset, when they have their biggest meal of the day. It is customary during the latter part of Ramadan for children to march through the streets singing and collecting donations of nuts and sweets to eat during this holy time.

As Ramadan ends, Muslims celebrate Eid al-Fitr, a three-day holiday full of feasting, visiting, and gift exchanges.

Religious Celebrations

The most important modern holiday in Yemen is the Day of National Unity, celebrated on May 22. This marks the day that the two Yemens were united into the Republic of Yemen. There are many parades, dancing, singing, and sporting events.

Some cities still celebrate some of the holidays that were observed before the unification. These celebrations depend on the region. The south celebrates Revolution Day on October 14 to mark the beginning of the revolution against British rule. The north recognizes September 26 as its Revolution Day, when the Yemen Arab Republic was established.

Every September an autumn festival is held in the area of Jawf, bordering Oman. This is an ancient tradition that celebrates the end of the first monsoon rains, which are so important to the farmers. There is folk dancing and music and plenty of food.

Many festivals are held during the harvest of the date palm in mid-July. The date palm has been glorified since pre-Islamic times when villagers celebrated the arrival of fresh dates.

Did You Know?

The date palm was a symbol of beauty and victory. Its likeness was seen on temples, palaces, city gates, and the crowns of kings.

Arts

Many forms of creative talent flourish in Yemen. Yemenis are known for their love of poetry, oral storytelling, fine metalwork, and architecture. At most gatherings there is some form of music and dance.

Traditional Crafts

Yemen is famous for its beautiful silver jewelry. Combining silver with coral, amber, agate, and glass, jewelry makers design elaborate headpieces, earrings, belts, and rings. Today people who live in the cities are choosing to wear gold more than the traditional jewelry.

Because the Qur'an forbids using pictures of living things, Muslims have created geometric designs to decorate their jewelry and pottery.

Daggers that are worn by most men are handmade by Yemeni artisans. The design varies by region, tribe, and social standing. Some daggers have bone or wooden handles and are kept in a leather sheath. The elite classes carry daggers with ornate silver handles in an embroidered or wooden sheath.

Visual Arts

The works of Yemeni artists are not well known outside of the Arabian Peninsula. To give these artists exposure to a wider audience, an exhibition of Yemeni art was held in London in November 2000.

The walls, doors, and windows of Yemeni homes are decorated with intricate geometric patterns. Many houses in Sana'a have elaborate window designs that resemble lace.

Performing Arts

Yemen has a long history of dance traditions. Each community has its own unique dance. A dance that distinguishes one tribe from another is called a *bara*. These dances are only performed outdoors by men. The number of dancers, the music, the steps, and how the dagger is held all show which tribe the men are from.

The Yemenis love music. They play the *oud,* a Middle Eastern lute, and the *simsimiya,* a five-string harp-like instrument that is popular along the Red Sea coast. Reed windpipes and various kinds of drums are used throughout the country. Accompanied by these instruments, Yemenis sing religious songs, poetry chants, and ballads. Military songs were popular during the 1960s.

GLOSSARY

allied having formed a union with another country to promote common interests

constitution a written document that tells what a country's laws are and how its people will be governed

desalination the process of removing salt from ocean water in order to produce drinking water or water for industrial use

expatriate a person living in a foreign country

gecekondus shanty towns that have sprung up on the outskirts of most Turkish cities

guerrillas armed fighters, usually those who are trying to overthrow their government

millets communities that shared the same religion during the Ottoman period

nationalists people who believe that their country or region should be independent

protectorate a country that depends upon a foreign country for protection

secular not related to religion

secularism the exclusion of religion from politics and public life

unification the act of uniting or making into a whole

wadi a permanent, often dry, riverbed in the desert that fills during the rainy season

BIBLIOGRAPHY

Arabic in Yemen. "Food and Mealtime Etiquette."
    <http://www.arabicinyemen.com/food.htm>

Baykal, Huseyin Azmi. "Silver Repoussage." *Antika: The Turkish Journal
    of Collectible Art,* vol. 11. 2/85. <http://www.mfa.gov.tr/
    grupc/cj/cja/silver.htm>

Committee to Protect Journalists. "Attacks on the Press 2002: United
    Arab Emirates." <http://www.cpj.org/attacks02/mideast02/uae.html>

Dialog Foundation. "Enamelled Tile Making."
    <http://www.dialogfoundation.org/culture/tile.html>

Dosti, Rose. *Mideast & Mediterranean Cuisines.* Tucson, AZ: Fisher
    Books, 1993.

Encyclopedia Britannica. "Yemen." 9/03. <http://www.britannica.com/
    eb/article?eu=119546>

Göksell, Ali Esad. "Ramazan Meals in the Ottoman Times." *Skylife.*
    1/97. <http://www.atamanhotel.com/ramazan.html>

Güvenç, Bozkurt. "History of Turkish Education." *Council of Higher
    Education of the Republic of Turkey.* <http://www.yok.gov.tr/
    webeng/histedu/histtredu.html>

Mailos, Tess. *The Complete Mediterranean Cookbook.* Boston: Charles E
    Tuttle, 1996.

Metz, Helen Chapin, ed. *Persian Gulf States: Country Studies.* Washington, DC: Federal Research Division, Library of Congress, 1994. <http://lcweb2.loc.gov/frd/cs/aetoc.html>

————.*Turkey: Country Studies.* Washington, DC: Federal Research Division, Library of Congress, 1996. <http://lcweb2.loc.gov/frd/cs/trtoc.html>

Morgan, Tabitha. "Turkey's 'Men-Only' Politics Angers Women." *BBC News.* 9/22/02. <http://news.bbc.co.uk/1/hi/world/europe/2274111.stm>

Pelham, Nick. "Yemen Resumes War on Al-Qaeda." *BBC News.* 2/14/02. <http://news.bbc.co.uk/2/hi/middle_east/1820918.stm>

Republic of Turkey. "Turkish Embassy." <http://www.turkishembassy.org >

Salloum, Habeeb. *From the Lands of Figs and Olives.* Brooklyn, NY: Interlink Books, 1995.

Sheehan, Sean. *Turkey.* New York: Marshall Cavendish, 1993.

Spenser, William. *The Land and People of Turkey.* New York: Lippincott, 1990.

Turkey. "The Real Story of Sweets: Beyond the Baklava." <www.asu.net/turkiye/tr_ye_10.htm>

Turkey's First Sports Portal. "The Historical Importance of Anatolia from the Point of View of Living Things and Its Biological Diversity." <http://www.sporum.gov.tr/English/Turkey/Interests/Wildlife.asp>

Turkish Cultural Foundation. <http://www.turkishculture.org/>

United States Geological Survey. "Minerals Information." 6/24/02.
    <http://minerals.usgs.gov/minerals/>

VolareTour. "About Turkey: Flora and Fauna."
    <http://www.volaretour.com/infocenter/turkey_flora.html>

Whitcraft, Melissa. *The Tigris and Euphrates Rivers.* New York: Franklin
    Watts, 1999.

CUMULATIVE INDEX

Note: Page numbers in *italics* indicate illustrations and captions.